THE
DREAMER'S
JOURNAL

To Write to the Author

If you wish to contact the author or would like more information about this book, please write to the author in care of Llewellyn Worldwide and we will forward your request. Both the author and publisher appreciate hearing from you and learning of your enjoyment of this book and how it has helped you. Llewellyn Worldwide cannot guarantee that every letter written to the author can be answered, but all will be forwarded. Please write to:

Barbara Moore
℅ Llewellyn Worldwide
2143 Wooddale Drive, Dept. 978-0-7387-1436-3
Woodbury, Minnesota 55125-2989, U.S.A.
Please enclose a self-addressed stamped envelope for reply,
or $1.00 to cover costs. If outside U.S.A., enclose
international postal reply coupon.

Many of Llewellyn's authors have websites with additional information and resources. For more information, please visit our website at http://www.llewellyn.com

THE
DREAMER'S
JOURNAL

TEXT BY
BARBARA MOORE

CARDS BY
HEIDI DARRAS

Llewellyn Publications
Woodbury, Minnesota

First Edition
First Printing, 2008

Book design and format by Donna Burch
Cover imagery from *Mystic Dreamer Tarot* cards © 2008 by Heidi Darras
Cover design by Gavin Dayton Duffy
Editing by Connie Hill
Tarot cards © 2008 by Heidi Darras
Llewellyn is a registered trademark of Llewellyn Worldwide, Ltd.

Library of Congress Cataloging-in-Publication Data
Moore, Barbara.
 The dreamer's journal / Barbara Moore. — 1st ed.
     p. cm.
  ISBN 978-0-7387-1436-3
  1. Tarot. I. Title.
  BF1879.T2D355   2008
  133.3'2424—dc22

                                                        2008018079

Llewellyn Publications
A Division of Llewellyn Worldwide, Ltd.
2143 Woodale Drive, Dept. 978-0-7387-1436-3
Woodbury, Minnesota 55125-2989, U.S.A.
www.llewellyn.com

Printed in the United States of America

Author's Acknowledgments

The *Mystic Dreamer Tarot* kit is the result of many talented people. Special thanks to Gavin, Donna, and Connie for making this package so beautiful, and, of course, Heidi for the inspiring art. Mark McElroy and Karen Mahony, your work has inspired me greatly; thank you for your contributions to the world of tarot.

Artist's Acknowledgments

I thank all the stock photographers who made it possible to create this deck. Without them, this deck wouldn't exist. All the models, the objects, the landscapes stocks deserve special appreciation; they were my muses, triggering my inspiration and imagination.

Thank you, too, to all the people in the DeviantArt community and friends who supported me during this whole process. Without their strength and encouragement, I would have never succeeded. They gave me the strength to make all these cards. They gave me courage when I struggled with a difficult card.

Thanks to the models who gave life to the cards:

Aaron R. Morgan, Alekxander Darras, Alexandra "Rena" Feehery, Alexis, Ana Cruz, Angela, Angelica Felis, Angie Lipovsek, Arsenal-Greenfeed, Ashley Bryrur, Becca, Blue Tigress, Brian Cooke, Caitlan McCollum, Carina Dejaegher, Cassandra Kirsch, Cheryl Fox, Christyl, Cobweb, Dana, Dany Lestat, David, Duncan Price, Elandria Broughton-Sheard, Elisabeth Siegl, Flavia Gabral, Gemma Bencini, Ida Larsen aka Mizzd, Jamie Lipovsek, Jennifer Owens, Jenny Neiman, Jessica Truscott, Joel Castleberry, Katherine Haig, Kenya, Li Vincent, Lindowyn, Liva Rutmane, Lorna Cowie, Marion Skydancer, Melissa Steele, Nadja, Nikolaos aka Lucretius, Oana Celina Noree Mihailescu, Oihane Molinero, Ominous, Paola Constant, Rachel Doherty, Rebecca Cusworth, Sabine Jungulaus, Sam, Sophie Collier, Stock Xchng, Tarun Sai Ravuri, and Tim.

And thank you to Llewellyn, Vanessa Wright, and Barbara Moore, for their patience and help through this unknown process toward publication.

Author's Dedication

As always, to Lisa, a merciless editor
and the supporter of dreams.

Artist's Dedication

For my husband and my son,
for their love and understanding
and for all their patience
as I spent so much time in the middle
of the night making these cards and other things
that are my hobby and my passion.

Contents

Author's Note

Although I have written several books for tarot decks, each one is always a new journey. Before pen hits paper, I spend time with the images. Each deck has its own personality and as the writer it is my job to express that personality. When I start writing, I never know for sure how it's going to turn out. Each deck brings its own joys and challenges. With each one my knowledge of tarot expands and my understanding of myself deepens.

Working with the *Mystic Dreamer Tarot* has been challenging and has brought about the most change in my understanding and knowledge. By nature, I am inclined to linear structure. *The Gilded Tarot* spoke to me of the numerological connections between the Major Arcana and the four suits of the Minor Arcana. That is, the Aces related to the Magician, the Twos to the High Priestess, etc. The *Mystic Faerie Tarot* brought its own narrative structure; each suit told a story. The *Mystic Dreamer* did not speak to me of structure.

In her Artist's Note, Heidi speaks of using the moon as a recurring symbol. She says that she uses it because it stands for intuition, creativity, magic, and mystery. She uses it to remind us to pay attention to details, to look closely before jumping to conclusions. The moon, after all, can hide as much as it reveals. She uses symbols meant to inspire intuitive personal reactions and interpretations. She has created a deck that doesn't want any linear structure.

What a challenge and a journey for me. Luckily, her images are based on traditional tarot card meanings, so there is some underlying foundation. Some symbols she included because of specific connotations. Others are there to speak to individual readers. As the writer, I had to find the balance between providing enough information for a beginner to read the cards and allowing enough space for personal, intuitive interpretations.

This challenge also caused me to review how much of myself and my own beliefs enter the card meanings. Looking over my previous works, I see a lot of advice for the reader. Each card provides not only a meaning but also my opinion of how that meaning should be applied in the reader's life. This deck would not let me do that. It demanded that I give a basic, traditional interpretation without judgment or commentary, providing advice only when the card itself suggested it.

Those familiar with the aforementioned books will notice another difference: the inclusion of reversed meanings. When I began this project I did not intend to include them. However, in some bizarre, unexplainable way, the reversed meanings started flowing from the card into my mind and onto the paper...even before the upright meanings. After a few false starts, I gave in and let the cards tell me what they wanted written about them.

Another change from my usual practice pertains to the questions that readers ask when doing a tarot reading. I have always believed that people should be encouraged to ask empowering questions and take a proactive approach to their lives. This deck taught me that despite my good intentions, it is not my place to say how people should do that. This deck taught me to allow people to ask the questions they want to ask.

As I said, each deck has a personality. Generally, I expect my writing to reflect that personality. For the *Mystic Dreamer* I was prepared for mystical, lovely prose. I was, therefore, surprised when I found the writing to be quite unembellished and more matter-of-fact.

After much internal struggle, I came to terms with my role as the writer. It was to provide just enough foundation to let readers feel secure and enough room for their own intuition to speak.

May your journey be as interesting as mine.

Artist's Note

Call it faith...

Five years ago, my son was born. He didn't like that I cleaned downstairs while he was sleeping. So I discovered the Internet and a program called PaintshopPro8. I started to make cards from it, just for fun, cutting and pasting photos and adding little effects. While I was on the computer, my son slept for three hours instead of his usual thirty minutes. So I had some time for myself. I started to relax and have fun. And I began an adventure that I never would have predicted.

In 2004, I joined DeviantArt (DA), an online art gallery. I always was a little bit creative and liked to paint, but I hadn't touched a brush in eight years, so finding PaintshopPro8 and DA was the beginning of a very intense creative process for me. I spent hours and hours improving my skills, just for the fun of it. And sometimes I felt like I was making up for lost time. I never went to art school, something I always regretted. This was my way of nurturing the creative spark I'd always had.

In November 2006, I was manipulating another piece of art, a strange one, and when it was finished it looked like the Tower from a tarot deck. So I started on another one, to see if it was time to create my own personal deck, and the Moon was born. The third card was the Sun, and before I knew it I was making the complete Major Arcana.

If the first three cards had failed, this deck would never have been born. After making the Major Arcana, I was planning to stop, but then the people on DA started to ask if I would create the full deck, and I just felt a big urge to do so.

I knew that it would be challenging and an important lesson in patience in completing a project.

I had always wanted to create a deck from the moment I read about them when I was seventeen. I couldn't find a deck that resonated with me, so I promised myself that one day I would make one. Tarot decks are fascinating. They tell stories in each little card and they also give advice. They are stubborn, with a mind of their own.

I knew my dream deck would be emotional. I wanted to reveal the hidden emotion in each card. But I also wanted to eliminate the symbols from the Bible, as much as I could, to make the images more up-to-date and accessible. I also wanted the deck to have an aura of mystery and dreaminess. Some symbols took on special importance and are repeated through the deck. Ravens and other birds show up often, as does the moon; I have a particular connection with the moon.

In dreams, ravens symbolize the secrets of the subconscious, showing us things that we would prefer not to know. They represent a feeling of foreboding, an important message, or something in our lives that needs attention.

The moon stands for intuition, emotions, creativity, inspiration, and it can evoke a feeling of magic and mystery. The moon tells us to pay attention to the details before jumping to conclusions. It can reveal inner peace and feelings of serenity. Most of the moons in this deck are full, which tells us that we need to trust our instincts and intuition to reach our goals.

I always had the feeling that I was just a tool while I was creating the deck. I couldn't say, "Now I shall the make the

Fool," because I always ended up with a different card. I had to work by intuition. I saw a model and started, that's it. Only after I was finished did I know if it would be a wand, a sword, a pentacle, or a cup. I learned so much as I created this deck. I learned to look closer at each card, discovering their hidden mysteries, and yet I still don't know everything about them.

The deck itself is photo-manipulated, which means that the cards were created from lots of different photos. Different pieces were used to create new landscapes. Also 3D programs like Daz3D and Vue d'esprit helped me create the details in the cards, along with a little bit of digital painting. It is really a high-tech version of cutting and pasting with some embellishments.

I never expected that people would like the deck so much and even want to have it for their own readings and use. I was surprised when I received emails from so many who liked the deck. And I never expected or even dreamed that the deck would be published. It was something that was far away from my mind, but I should have known that the deck wouldn't be pleased to remain stored on my computer and would demand more.

So this is the story of my *Mystic Dreamer Tarot*. It's been one big adventure, one dream come true that I would never have dreamed could happen.

Introduction

Dark, shadowy, and surreal, the images of the *Mystic Dreamer Tarot* invite us to enter their mysterious scenes. Here we can lose ourselves amongst moments of joy, fear, action, and contemplation as we face our past, our present, and our future. We are forced to look carefully and imaginatively. If we look with our eyes and with our intuition, we will find that more is illuminated than hidden—but only if we seek carefully.

We dream while sleeping and in order to sleep, we calm our bodies and our minds. The *Mystic Dreamer Tarot* demands the same calm approach. To hear the messages hidden in dark corners of these cards, we must slow down, relax, and allow our imagination to flow. These cards are not always what they seem—and therein lies their unique and extraordinary power. We might see a bright object in a card but miss the symbol hiding in the corner. Does the bright object represent a distraction? Perhaps we are letting something in our life distract us from the real issue. We might see a dark card but miss the tiny illuminated symbol in the background. Are we overcome with pessimism and refusing to see the light that guides our path?

This book will serve as a map and a small flashlight for the adventure through this dreamscape. It provides basic information for understanding the tarot and a step-by-step guide to doing an effective reading. Tarot journals, those most effective tools of tarot study and dream work, are discussed, along with helpful journaling suggestions. There are lots of spreads for readings on a variety of issues and questions. Techniques for using this deck for dream interpretation add another dimension of usefulness. And finally, the cards are explored and basic meanings provided. But this book is only a map and only a small flashlight. Those who read this book and those who deal these cards will create their own journey. And each experience will be unique.

Tarot Deck Basics

We randomize a deck of cards by shuffling. Whether we are playing a game or preparing to do a reading, we shuffle the cards, deal or lay them out, and play or interpret the hands we are dealt. But before the cards are shuffled, they are created in a specific order. If we understand the order, we can more easily understand the individual cards and how they interact in the game or the reading.

The cards in a tarot deck are divided into several categories. These categories shape the meanings of the cards. The deck has seventy-eight cards. Twenty-two of these have roman numerals and names, such as "II, The High Priestess" or "VI, The Lovers," although most people refer to them by their names only, not their numbers. These twenty-two cards are called the Major Arcana, meaning important secrets. We all have faced situations that changed us or our lives in significant ways. We've all experienced events over which we had little or no control. Various Major Arcana cards, such as the Chariot, the Tower, and the Wheel of Fortune, reflect these life-changing experiences. The Major Arcana is also associated with messages from the spiritual realm. As such, cards like the Magician, Temperance, and the Hermit provide advice. The names of these cards give hints about the cards' meaning. For example, the Wheel of Fortune is about a major change in a situation, the Hermit is about withdrawing, and Temperance is about moderation.

The remaining fifty-six cards are called the Minor Arcana. Unlike the Majors, these cards represent everyday concerns. The Minor Arcana is divided into four suits, like a deck of playing cards. Instead of hearts, clubs, spades, and diamonds, the suits are wands, cups, swords, and pentacles. Each suit has elemental associations and meanings. Wands are associated with fire and show our passions, our drives, our careers, and our projects. Cups are associated with water and deal with our emotions, our creativity, our relationships, and our loves. Swords are associated with air and focus on our intellect, our thought processes, our problems, and our challenges. Pentacles are associated with earth and are concerned with our money, our resources, our creations, our body, and our health.

Each suit contains an ace through ten, and these cards represent situations. Each suit also includes four court cards: page, knight, queen, and king. The court cards represent people. With the court cards, keep in mind that people are complex and likely exhibit several or even many of the court card personalities throughout their day. Court cards represent only one aspect of a person—the part that pertains to the reading at hand. For example, a woman holding an executive position with a large company may be a King of Swords at work, a Queen of Pentacles when she's at home with her family, and a Page of Cups if she takes an evening art class. Although the figures on the court cards are clearly male or female, they can represent people of either gender.

Now that we have these cards, what do we do with them? Historically, tarot cards were used to play card games and, in parts of Europe, they still are. Most people are familiar with tarot cards being used to tell fortunes. In recent decades, creative and innovative tarot experts and enthusiasts have discovered many new applications for the cards. For example, you can find books, articles, workshops, and classes that show how to use the cards for therapy, brainstorming, problem-solving, creative writing, mediation, pathworking, magic, rituals, dream work, journaling, self-improvement, past life exploration, and artistic inspiration. Tarot opens up an ever-expanding world of possibilities. The *Mystic Dreamer* can be used for any of these activities. The most popular thing to do with tarot cards is, of course, a reading.

Notes

_____

_____

_____

_____

_____

_____

_____

_____

_____

_____

_____

_____

_____

_____

_____

_____

_____

Reading the Cards

Most people buy tarot decks for the express purpose of doing readings, also known as fortunetelling or divination. Reading the cards isn't difficult. This section will explain how to do a reading step by step. Remember that your readings will become smoother with practice. There is a process to reading, which can be explained here—but there is also an art to it, which will only come as you become more confident of the basic meanings and as you develop your own intuitive interpretations of the cards. As you discover your favorite spreads and interpretive nuances, such as how certain cards relate to each other, your own personal style will emerge. You may find that you have a knack for certain types of readings but find others more challenging. As you experiment with asking different types of questions, you will figure out what kind of wording brings you the best results.

Doing a tarot reading can be as complex and ritualistic as you like. You can include special cloths to lay the cards on, crystals, incense, candles, music, prayers, visualizations, or whatever else you like. All of these can add to the enjoyment of the experience and, depending on your beliefs and practices, can enhance your reading's accuracy and usefulness. Here, though, we are going to focus on the most basic elements of a reading.

The first thing to do is determine what question you want answered. Think it over and make it as clear and specific in your mind as you can. The question can be as simple as "What do I need to know about ____?" or it can be more complex, as long as it is clear in your mind. If it helps (and it usually does), write it down.

After you know what you want to ask, you need to pick a spread you want to use. A spread, also called a layout, is how you intend to lay out the cards. A very common spread is this three-card layout:

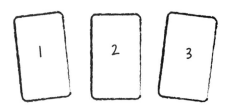

Each position is assigned a particular meaning. In this case, card one represents the past, card two represents the present, and card three represents the future.

As you select a spread, keep in mind your question. Look at the position meanings and see if they make sense in terms of your question. As you consider different spreads, you may be inspired to reword your question.

I should note here that I've seen people read without spreads. They just lay down the cards and stop when they feel like it and then they read the cards. This has always impressed me. Unfortunately, despite my best efforts, I have not mastered this yet. However, this deck is suited for such free-flowing readings and I've been enjoying experimenting with this reading style. Lay down some cards and let a story unfold. But if you prefer a little structure, in the next chapter you'll find a collection of spreads covering a variety of situations.

The question is settled, the spread selected—now it's time to take your future in your hands and shuffle the cards. Shuffle them however you like. You can take some of the cards and turn them around so that reversed cards are incorporated into your deck. However, it has been my experience that cards somehow get reversed whether I do that or not. Unlike playing cards, tarot card images have a top and a bottom. Reversed cards are cards that are upside down in relation to the other cards. When you are done, you can cut the deck or not. You can deal off the top or fan the cards out and pick each card randomly. While there is no agreement in the tarot community about what is the best method, there is *some* consensus that once you find your favorite way, do it the same every time. The sense of ritual or habit does have a way of focusing the mind and preparing it for what follows.

After the cards are shuffled, lay them out according to the spread you've selected. Because a reading is about interpreting the cards, their positions, and their relationship to each other, lay the cards face up so you can see all of them.

Now comes the interpretation of the spread; this is the heart of any reading. An overview of the cards, ignoring their positions, gives the first bits of information.

First, scan for Major Arcana cards and for the suits. A predominance of any of these indicates the focus of the reading. Major Arcana indicate that the reading will have particular significance. Likewise, cups would indicate that emotions are playing an important role, swords show the importance of thinking or a challenging situation, wands point to energy and drive, and pentacles suggest the physical realm. For example, if a reading about changing your career has many Major Arcana cards, you can be sure there are significant issues involved. If a reading about a relationship has no cups but several swords, keep your eyes open for trouble.

The numbers on the cards give the next layer of data. Aces, twos, and threes indicate the beginning of a cycle; fours, fives, and sixes show the middle; sevens, eights, and nines suggest that the cycle is winding down; and tens represent the end of a cycle. For example, say you are reading about selling your house. You would expect different cards to show up to indicate whether you were just getting ready to put it on the market, if showings were being booked and open houses arranged, or if bids were coming in or negotiations going on.

Check for court cards. They represent people involved in the events at hand or a specific aspect of your personality that is influencing the situation. Several court cards in a reading about a job you've applied for could indicate many other candidates or lots of people involved in the decision-making process.

Look for reversed cards. Reversed cards have their own meanings, but if a reading has a predominance of reversed cards, that can have significance. Generally, it indicates that a situation is blocked or delayed, or that nothing is what it seems.

Once you have this preliminary foundation of information, interpret the individual cards in terms of their position in the spread. The card meanings in this book are written as if referring to the present moment, so you will have to adjust them if they are in, for example, the past position or in an outcome position or in relation to you or someone else. For example, the Three of Wands can mean: "Because you've done your work well, you can expect to see signs of success." If this card shows up in the past position, it would mean that you've done your work well, and that you are, or soon will be, enjoying success.

Now you will look at the cards in relation to each other, keeping in mind the meanings of their positions. Your personal or intuitive interpretations will come into play here, as well as the images themselves. Notice colors, the directions that people are facing, pillars that create blocks or boundaries, etc. All the cards in this book include questions to stimulate your intuition, which should come in handy at this point.

You are ready now to interpret your reading as a whole. Incorporating all the information you've gathered, use the positions of the spread as an outline to frame your answer.

More than likely, your answer will be about something in the future. One thing to keep in mind about the future is that it can change. Your readings will show the probable end result if all things remain as they are. Remember that something outside your control can change the way a situation plays out. Likewise, actions you take can alter the course of events for better or worse—a good thing to keep in mind if you are less than pleased with the current outcome.

Keeping a Tarot Journal

Most tarot authors advise keeping a journal. Most people may begin keeping one but then don't continue. So why do authors and teachers keep suggesting it? Because it really is the best way to learn the cards and improve your reading skills. Even those with natural psychic or intuitive talent can hone their abilities by keeping a journal.

To develop a better understanding of the cards, keep a notebook with a few pages devoted to each card. Below are some ideas to inspire your journaling sessions. By doing these exercises, you'll learn the basic card meanings, what personal and intuitive messages are in the card for you, what sorts of real-life events and situations you associate with each card, and how the cards work together. You will learn the cards in a more concrete way, not just theoretically. Pick the ones that sound fun or inspiring and let your intuition guide you. You might be surprised at some of the discoveries you'll make—about the cards and about yourself.

1. Pick a card (randomly, or you can work your way through the entire deck in an orderly manner), read the interpretations and write down your thoughts. What parts of the interpretation ring true to you? What parts do you disagree with? Why?

2. Answer the questions included in this book. Try revisiting some of the cards and see if your answers change. How do those answers enhance or alter the meaning of the card for you?

3. Look at the images and see what comes to your mind. Explore how those ideas interact with the interpretations given in the book.

4. Make a timeline of the milestones in your life. Match Major Arcana cards to those events.

5. At the end of an ordinary day, pick some Minor Arcana cards that illustrate what happened to you that day.

6. For the court cards, think of a person, either someone you know, a celebrity, or a character from a movie, TV show, or book who reminds you of that card.

7. Think of ways that you express each of the court card personalities.

8. Separate your court cards from the rest of the deck. Shuffle the non-court card pile and draw three cards. Use those three to make up a story or situation. Pull a

court card. Imagine how that personality would react in that situation. If you really want a challenge, imagine how all the court cards would react in that situation.

9. Tarot expert Mary K. Greer teaches a fun exercise. Imagine you're walking along a beach and come upon a beach party. Everyone there is a court card personality. Crash the party and interact with everyone there.

10. Pull cards that seem similar to you, for example maybe the Empress and the Queen of Cups or Five of Swords and Seven of Swords. Write out how they are the same and how they are different. The next time the Seven of Swords comes up in a reading, pull the Five of Swords out of your deck and consider how the reading would be different if it came up instead. Noticing subtle differences like that can add precision and accuracy to your readings.

11. Experienced readers find that certain card combinations come up over and over again and take on specific meanings. For example, the Empress and the Ace of Wands in the same reading might mean pregnancy. The Magician reversed and the Chariot together could mean a vehicle is a bad deal or a lemon. As you do readings, if a combination comes up that seems particularly intriguing, note it down and watch for it in the future.

12. Another way to practice combinations is to think of specific situations, such as getting a job offer or getting called for a date or finding just the right item

when shopping, anything at all. Go through your deck and pull card combinations that represent those situations.

13. Write out every reading you do. Include the question asked, the spread used, the cards drawn, and your interpretation. Leave plenty of room to go back and make notes. After the situation has resolved, go back to your reading. Note where your interpretation was right and where it might have been off the mark. Using a different color pen is helpful. Figure out how you could have interpreted it differently now that you know what happened. How does this change or refine your interpretations for that card? Note those observations in your pages devoted to that card.

These techniques are not necessary to do a reading, but they can provide a better understanding of the cards and strengthen your confidence in your own reading skills.

Spreads

Spreads, also called layouts, are how the cards are laid out to do a reading. A spread is made up of card positions, and each position has a meaning. Using these positional meanings helps shape the interpretation of the card that falls there. Spreads can be small and simple, such as a one-card spread, or they can be large and complex, up to seventy-eight cards, although that's rare. In this section, you'll find first a collection of common, traditional spreads that have served tarot readers very well for decades—or longer. Following those are spreads that have been created to answer more specific concerns, such as love/romance and money, which are the most common types of questions that people use the tarot to answer.

Feel free to alter any of these spreads when necessary so that they most effectively and precisely address your situation. For example, there are a few spreads for deciding between two choices. If you have more than two choices, just add the appropriate number of cards to represent your circumstances. There is a job spread that has one position for the boss and one for co-workers. If you know that more than one boss or co-worker is involved, add more positions.

Traditional Spreads

One-Card Spread

This is the simplest spread, and can be used in an infinite number of ways. You simply ask your question and draw a card. The position in the one-card spread is always the answer to the question being asked. Below are some sample questions:

1. What do I need to know about _____?

2. What will happen if I _____?

3. How can I _____?

4. Where should I _____?

5. What do I need to be aware of today?

6. What should I do about _____?

Two-Card Spread

Two-card spreads are useful to a get a quick overview whenever your question focuses on two specific concerns or choices. If you have two options and want information about them and their potential outcomes think of one as option A, and the other as option B. Lay the cards out side by side:

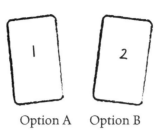

Option A   Option B

If you are facing a certain opportunity and want to know whether you should pursue it or not, use this variation:

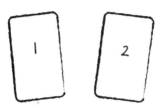

Should I?   Shouldn't I?

Three-Card Spread

The basic three-card spread is very popular, and has many variations. It's often a favorite of beginners, as there are enough cards to practice reading them together, but it is not overwhelming. More experienced readers like it, too, because it provides a quick but reliable reading. Sometimes you need advice, but don't have time for a longer spread.

Three-card spreads can be laid out in a number of ways. Some horizontal variations include:

1. Past
2. Present
3. Future

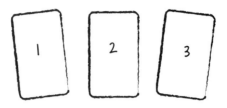

1. This morning
2. This afternoon
3. This evening

1. What I left behind
2. What I have
3. What I will get

Here are some horizontal variations with a slightly different layout:

1. You
2. What you have
3. What you need

1. The question
2. What to do
3. What not to do

One last horizontal variation:

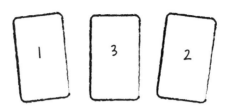

1. Choice A
2. Choice B
3. An option you haven't considered

1. You
2. Your partner
3. The relationship

A three-card spread can be laid out vertically:

1. Body
2. Mind
3. Spirit

Lay the cards in the following order:

1. Where I am
3. Where I want to be
2. How to get there

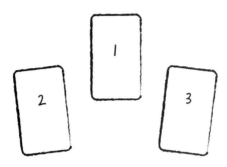

A triangle makes an interesting three-card layout.

1. The situation
2. Choice or option A
3. Choice or option B

1. You
2. The problem
3. The solution

Celtic Cross Spread

The Celtic Cross is probably the most well-known spread. In fact, some readers use it exclusively. It is an elegant and useful spread that provides in-depth information about a question.

1. You: this card represents you in terms of the question asked

2. Crossing: this card indicates the conflict, or what is crossing your path

3. Foundation: this card illustrates the basis or foundation of the situation

4. Past: this card shows influences from the past that are affecting the present situation

5. Immediate future: this card illustrates what is likely to happen next

6. Crown: this card represents the outcome you desire most in this situation

7. Yourself: this is your self-image; how you see yourself in the present situation

8. Environment: this card represents the influences of those around you; it can show how others see you in this situation

9. Hopes and fears: this card indicates either what you hope for or fear the most in this situation

10. Outcome: this card indicates the probable outcome if all things remain as they are.

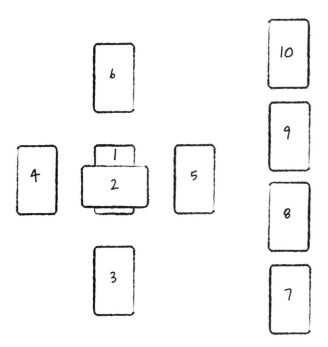

Astrological Spread

This spread is based on astrological charts used to plot horoscopes. It is a circle divided into twelve sections called houses. Each house represents an aspect of a person's life. This spread represents you at the time you do the reading. Many people like to do this reading once a year, either at the beginning of a new year or on their birthday.

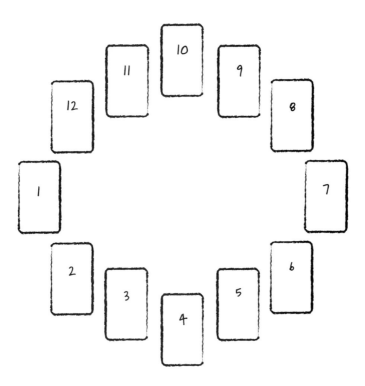

1. Your self-image and personality

2. Your value systems and material resources

3. Your siblings and communication

4. Your parents, your home, and family

5. Creativity, affairs of the heart, fun, and children

6. Work, responsibilities, and health

7. Partnership, both romantic and business

8. Sex, death, and shared money

9. Travel, higher education, spiritual connections

10. Your public image, vocation, and ambitions

11. Friends, hopes, goals, and wishes

12. Your inner self, dreams, secrets, the past

Two Paths Spread

This is one of my favorites. If you are facing a choice between two options, this spread gives you lots of information to help you make the best decision. Cards 2, 3, and 4 represent choice A and 5, 6, and 7 represent choice B.

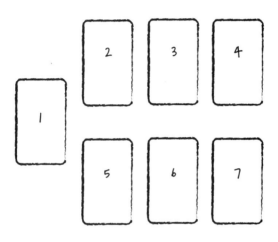

1. Where you are now

2 and 5: The benefits of each choice

3 and 6: The downsides of each choice

4 and 7: The probable outcomes of each path

Love and Romance Spreads*

Does He Love Me Spread

This spread provides insight into how your beau feels about you and the relationship. You can also do this reading about how you feel about him and the relationship. If you're ambitious, do it for both of you and compare the two readings.

You   The relationship

| 1 | 2 |

| 3 | 4 |

| 5 | 6 |

| 7 | 8 |

1. How he feels about you

3. What he thinks about you

5. What he loves best about you

7. What he doesn't love about you

2. His favorite aspect of the relationship

4. His least favorite aspect of the relationship

6. His hopes for the relationship

8. His fears regarding the relationship

* Text for these spreads is written from the feminine viewpoint; substitute gender as desired.

Will This Relationship Last Spread

This spread examines the strengths and weaknesses of the relationship. If the outcome indicates that it won't last, you can address some of the weaknesses and perhaps change the outcome.

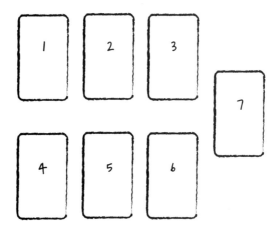

1, 2, 3: The strengths of the relationship

4, 5, 6: The weaknesses of the relationship

7: The probable outcome if everything remains as it is

Will I Find Love Spread

Use this spread if you are seeking romance. If love is in the wings, the spread can point you in the right direction. If love isn't in the immediate future, it can tell you what you need to know to change that.

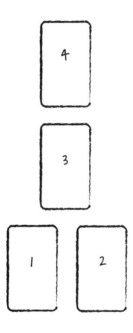

1. What do I need to know about finding love at present?

2. In what way am I ready or not ready for love?

3. What do I want from love?

4. Where can I find love?

Is He "The One" for Me Spread

This spread will help you understand how you feel about your current love and the relationship.

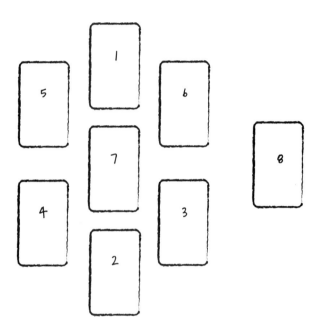

1. What's hot?

2. What's not?

3. How do you respond to him emotionally?

4. How do you respond to him physically?

5. How do you respond to him spiritually?

6. How do you respond to him intellectually?

7. What do you think of him?

8. The question you need to ask yourself.

What Do I Need to Know Spread

This spread gets used when someone feels like something is wrong with the relationship, or that the partner is being unfaithful. Cheating may be the immediate concern, but it springs from an inherent problem in the relationship. This spread can clue you in to what's wrong and how each of you choose to deal with it.

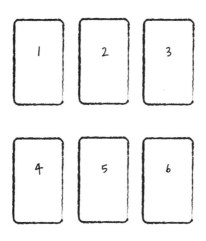

1. What do you get from him?
2. What do you not get from him?
3. If not him, where are you getting it?
4. What does he get from you?
5. What does he not get from you?
6. If not you, where is he getting it?

Money and Career Spreads

Getting Ready Spread

This spread will help you prepare for a job interview or review. It'll reveal your best assets and how to show them off while downplaying anything that won't help your cause.

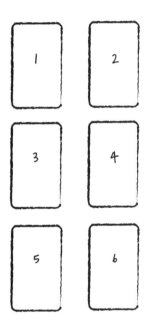

1. What the employers want from you

2. How you can highlight it

3. What they don't want from you

4. How you can minimize it

5. What they don't realize they want

6. How you can really "wow" them

Waiting for the Answer Spread

If you already went on the interview or had the review, this spread will tell you how it went.

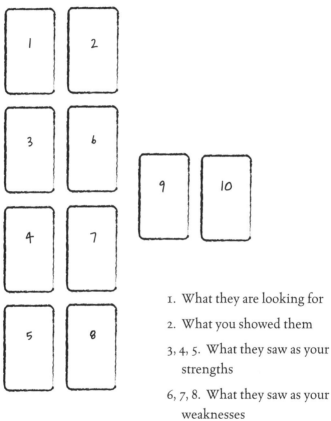

1. What they are looking for
2. What you showed them
3, 4, 5. What they saw as your strengths
6, 7, 8. What they saw as your weaknesses
9. Something you need to know about the situation
10. The probable outcome

Should I Take It Spread

If you've been offered a job and are wondering if you should accept it, this spread can help you decide. If you find yourself in the fortunate position of having two or more offers, do this for each and compare the results.

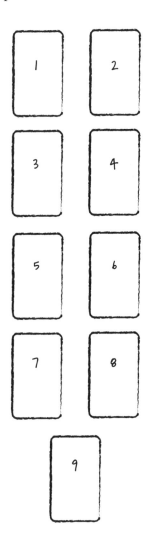

1. The best benefit for you
2. The biggest downside for you
3. What you'll love about the job
4. What you won't
5. What you'll appreciate about the boss
6. What you'll find most challenging about the boss
7. What you'll like about the co-workers
8. What will challenge you about the co-workers
9. What you need to know about this job

Notes

_____

_____

_____

_____

_____

_____

_____

Is Prosperity Coming My Way Spread

Looking for a little something extra to come your way? Find out what's in store. This spread depends on the number of your needs or wants. List them out before beginning. By way of example, let's say you listed three.

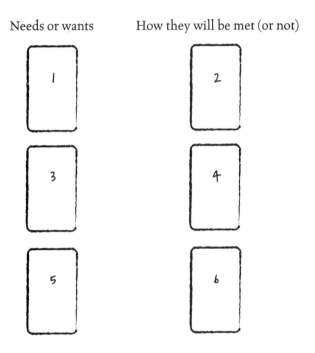

If the cards indicate that any of the needs won't be met, pull an extra card to find out if there is another resource that you could investigate.

Additional Spreads

Message from the Universe Spread

If you don't have a specific question, but feel like there is a part of your life that needs attention, use this spread as a kind of gauge or thermometer to see how you're doing in. Divide your cards into five piles: Major Arcana, wands, cups, swords, and pentacles. Shuffle each pile and set them facedown as shown below:

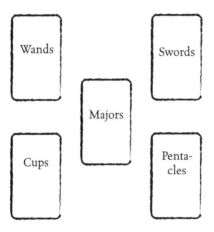

Turn over the top card in each pile.

The Major Arcana card represents your spiritual life
The wands card represents your work life.
The cups card represents your emotional life.
The swords card represents your intellectual life.
The pentacles card represents your physical life.

If any area seems to need attention, look at the card on the bottom of its pile for advice on what action to take.

What to Do Spread

If you are looking for a new direction for your life—a new job, a new place to live, a new project or hobby, a course of study—this spread can suggest an answer.

1, 2, 3. What you did in the past

10. The outcome

4, 5, 6. What you're doing now (or just finished doing)

11. The outcome

7, 8, 9. What you should do next

12. The probable outcome

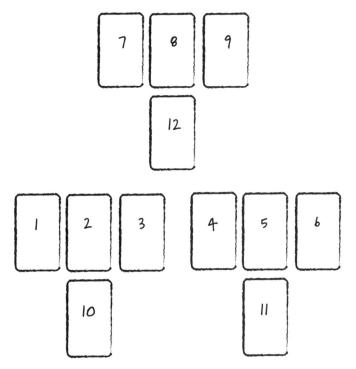

Working It Out Spread

If you've had an argument or disagreement with someone, this spread can point you toward a resolution. This layout should be customized as necessary to represent each point of the situation, argument, or disagreement. For an example, we'll say that you and your friend have three areas of contention.

1, 2, 3. Your point of view

4, 5, 6. The other person's point of view

7, 8, 9. How you can find common ground

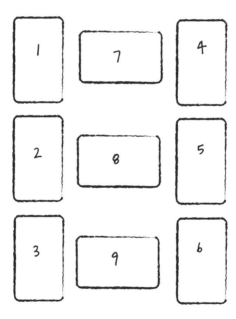

Notes

_____

_____

_____

_____

_____

_____

_____

_____

_____

_____

_____

_____

_____

_____

_____

_____

Dream Work

Dreams are a mysterious part of our lives. They can amuse, inspire, frustrate, or terrify us. And while we don't know everything about dreams—where they come from, what causes them, what their purpose is—many people agree that some dreams have more significance than others. Sometimes dreams mean something; they are messages from our subconscious.

Dreams use symbols, just like tarot cards, to speak to the conscious mind. Sometimes our conscious mind needs a little help with these symbols. This is where tarot cards can help. One theory of how tarot works is this: all the answers that we seek are within us. The trouble is that the "within us" part communicates largely with symbols. Tarot cards feature images and symbols that resonate with our subconscious or inner self. Tarot cards also have structure, numbers, names, and basic meanings that give our conscious mind something to hold onto. The cards help build a bridge between our conscious and subconscious minds. Because of this unique characteristic, the cards can help with dream interpretation.

Here we'll look at three methods of using the *Mystic Dreamer Tarot* to help understand dreams. If you keep a dream diary, add these readings to your dream entries. Another benefit of using tarot for dream interpretation is that you may find that over time your dreams start incorporating aspects of the tarot, making the dreams easier for you to understand. Also, you will likely find that, by writing about your dreams and the cards together, your dreams will lend deeper understanding to the cards.

Dream Reading Random

This is a technique I learned from the esteemed tarot author Rachel Pollack. Think about your dream in terms of sections or scenes. Write out the sections in order. This works best if you have between three and seven sections. Randomly draw a card for each section and lay them out in order. Use the images and meanings of the cards to help interpret each scene.

Dream Reading Selected

This technique is a variation of the previous one. As described above, write out your dream in sections. Go through your deck and, ignoring the names, pick cards that look like each part of your dream. The cards won't look exactly like your dream, but find an element, feeling, or symbol on the card that you can associate with a scene from your dream.

Lay the cards out in order, using them to interpret each scene.

Dream Spread

Interpreting symbols is one aspect of dream work. Once you've done either of the dream readings, this spread can help you understand why the message was necessary and how to apply it in your life.

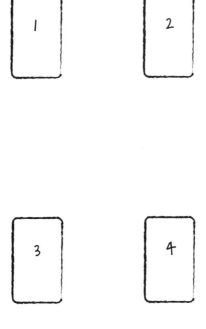

1. What specific event, situation, reaction, emotion, etc., is this dream about?

2. What blocked the message from my conscious mind?

3. What is the most important message that I should take from this dream?

4. How do I apply that message in my waking life?

The Major Arcana

The cards of the Major Arcana have intriguing titles, like the High Priestess and the Hierophant; frightening titles, like the Hanged Man and Death; and familiar names, like the Sun and the Moon. Whether intriguing, frightening, or familiar, these cards will lead you on a wondrous journey as you explore your future, your hopes, and your fears. These cards represent important events, the hand of fate, and wise advice. Listen to their messages with your heart and your mind.

The Fool, wearing black embellished in colorful ruffles and bells, dances on the edge of a cliff. She is reveling in a particular moment in time, one where all possibilities exist, that brief moment when all choices seem available. There is potential and danger present; she is, after all, standing on a dangerous precipice. The cards, representing her choices, float around her. The bag attached to her staff is filled with everything she will need, no matter what she encounters. The light from her lantern illuminates and casts shadows. Her dog can give encouragement and warning, if necessary.

A raven perches on a sign, which the Fool seems to ignore. She seems, instead, to prefer a more random method or, perhaps, a more intuitive one to pick her path.

This card indicates being at a crossroads. There are a variety of paths you can choose and the Fool suggests making an intuitive decision even if it seems illogical. This is a moment for faith and trust, in yourself and in the Universe. Follow your heart and embrace whatever comes your way.

If reversed, this card warns of making a foolish decision. You may be so focused on the future or your dreams that you are unaware of the danger signs right at your feet. Take the time to look around you, heeding signals that may help you make a wise choice.

Use your intuition

Which card will she pick and how will she decide?

What does the sign say?

What does she carry in her bag?

The Magician, with one hand raised to the heavens and one extended toward the earth, is a card of making dreams a reality. Before her are a pentacle, a chalice, a wand, and a sword, representing the four elements and the four suits of the Minor Arcana. These symbols bring to mind the aces of each suit, which contain both the energy of the suit and a window of opportunity to use that energy. They also show the creative process. The wand, or fire, is the creative spark, the initial concept of an idea, and the will to make it happen. The cup, or water, is the beginning of the dream or vision for the idea. The sword, or air, is the plan for the idea. The pentacle, or earth, is the idea becoming real. The Magician manages all this so effortlessly it does appear as magic.

This card indicates that it is time to focus on your goals, applying your determination and skill to achieve those goals. Everything you need is available and you have the ability necessary. Move forward with confidence because this card suggests success in your endeavors. This is a magical moment filled with potential just waiting to be realized.

If reversed, this card warns of potential deception. Beware of someone promising more than he can deliver. The Magician can also be a charlatan. Be careful, too, of tricking yourself. You may be convinced that your plan is good, but you might be missing a needed element or your plan may have unanticipated consequences.

Use your intuition

Of the four elements, the wand is the largest and appears most active (it is glowing). Also there are two candles, which also represent fire. What do these symbols say about the importance of will in achieving a goal?

What does the white robe signify?

Are the ravens in the background taking her wishes to heaven or bringing her inspiration or something else altogether?

The High Priestess is a mysterious card and represents secret knowledge, both revealed and hidden. The banner behind her is hiding something, but the image of the tree with its fruits of knowledge hint at what lies behind. She holds a glowing fruit, a shining bit of wisdom, but we are uncertain what it means. The moon at her feet and head show that this wisdom is shadowy and perhaps changing; it is best understood intuitively. In fact, intuition is vital to receiving the High Priestess' wisdom. The scroll on her lap promises explanation and understanding, if only she will share it. The black and white pillars are the negative and positive aspects of life. That the banner of knowledge hangs between them might suggest that usually the truth is neither black nor white, but lies somewhere in between.

This card is about knowledge that you need and that can be revealed. This knowledge is beyond logic. You must access and trust your intuition if you hope to understand it. Refrain from action for a while and instead take the time to search within yourself for the wisdom you need to move on. It could also mark the beginning of a personal spiritual journey. On a mundane level, it suggests sharing knowledge and not keeping secrets.

If reversed, this card warns of knowledge withheld. You may be seeking something that you are not meant to know. Perhaps someone is keeping something from you that you need to know. It could even be that you have knowledge that needs to remain secret, at least for now.

Use your intuition

On the banner, along with the tree, is a spiral staircase. Where does it lead and what does it mean?

On both pillars are figures holding something up. On the black one, the figure appears to be struggling, while on the white one the figure is standing gracefully upright. What does this signify?

What is behind the banner?

Sitting calmly on her throne, the Empress holds aloft a glowing wand in one hand, while the wheat sheaf in her other hand points toward the earth. In this way, she reminds us of the Magician. Like the Magician, the Empress is a card of creation. The emphasis here, though, is more passive and organic. The Empress' creation is connected to the cycles of life and the seasons. For her, life begins, grows, and dies. She nurtures creation through all those phases. She honors and respects both life and death, as they are really part of the same continuum. Unlike the Magician, who exerts control over his creation, the Empress lets the life cycle set the pace. The twelve stars in her crown represent the solar year and the field around her shows her concern with all growing things. She is the quintessential mother and is shown here pregnant.

This card shows a time of natural growth. Your role is to nurture without forcing or neglecting your project. Pay attention to where you are in the cycle of your project or situation and take the proper steps. There is great potential for abundance if good care is given. This may require action on your part or it may require a time of waiting.

If reversed, this card can indicate a couple of things. First, there is the possibility of too much nurturing and a danger of smothering something or someone. Second, you may be trying to rush a situation, creation, or project. The advice here is to back off and let nature take its course.

Use your intuition

The Empress, who is pregnant, is wearing black armbands. What do they signify?

What is the building in the background?

Does the hunting eagle by the water represent life or death?

The Emperor, a true symbol of leadership and power, sits on top of the earth. The sun and the moon float in the sky over his shoulders, as if waiting for his directions to either rise or set. His solid stone throne indicates the sturdy foundation he has built. It is topped with two ram's heads, the sign of Aries and so of strength, intelligence, and leadership. The Emperor uses the self-conscious mind and reason to create and build. He knows that even reason can benefit from the occasional message brought from beyond or within by way of intuition, which is why a raven is also present. Although not given to daydreams, he is a man of vision. He knows what he wants, what is needed, and how do it. Once he has created his empire, his role is to maintain it and rule it wisely. He does need to exercise caution against becoming a tyrant. There is also the danger that this man of action may find his throne to be a trap. Creating an empire is one thing; taking care of it is another.

This card is about being in control. You are, or should be, in charge of your life, your environment, your body, your temper, your actions. You, and you alone, should be in control of your life at this time. The card gives you permission to be assertive, brave, and bold. If you have already built a solid foundation, this card indicates that your goals will be realized. This card could also represent a leader that you admire and want to follow.

If reversed, this card suggests too much control, being aggressive and dictatorial for the sake of exercising power over others. Or you could be pushing yourself too hard by sheer force of will, but ignoring your heart. It can also represent an achievement that becomes oppressive.

Use your intuition

Are those white feathers on the Emperor's hat? What do they signify?

He is looking off into the distance. What does he see?

His wand is flaming. Why?

Seated casually between two pillars and two burning can-dles is the Hierophant. His resemblance to the High Priestess is striking. They are both interested in knowledge. However, while her knowledge is secret and esoteric, he is concerned with bringing divine wisdom down to earth. He does have a connection to the divine and otherworldly wis-dom, as evidenced by the two ravens in attendance. How-ever, his role is to speak that wisdom with a human voice, without being oblique or mysterious. This is symbolized by the orbs, representing the moon, lying on the floor at the base of the pillars. His hand is raised in a combination of blessing and beckoning, as if inviting students to come near. The cross behind him and the one next to him represent the intersecting of the divine and the worldly, the subconscious and conscious.

This card indicates a perfect balance of belief with practice. It is a good omen if you are facing a problem, as it indicates that you know the solution, but you need to find a way to put it into practice. If you are asked to teach, this card reminds you to be a good teacher, always seeking to make wisdom clear to any students. It can also indicate that you should seek a teacher for yourself, perhaps a formal or semi-formal course of study. Maybe the Hierophant is asking you to imagine what your life would be like if you lived by what you believe.

If reversed, this card suggests stubborn bullheadedness, particularly in areas of beliefs and their application in day-to-day life. You may be in a rut, unable to see new things or find useful ways to apply your beliefs in the real world. Consider giving up some routines and trying something new.

Use your intuition

There is a chalice on the floor on the far left. What is in it?

Something is carved in the stone behind the Hierophant. What is it and what does it mean?

The Hierophant wears boots, as if he's traveled a great deal. How does experience change the way you practice what you believe?

Aman and a woman cling together as they float above the earth. Between them is a chalice with a sword in it and nearby is a rose. The rose and chalice represent the couple's love, but the sword has separated them. Behind them are two trees. One tree has twelve flames indicating the twelve signs of the zodiac. The other tree is none other than the Tree of the Knowledge of Good and Evil. A huge moon rises over the scene, representing a kind of guardian spirit. It's a touching scene, but more representative than literal, for while this card may be about lovers, it can also be about other things. This card is mainly about choices. The man represents the conscious mind; the woman, the subconscious; and the moon, our higher self. We can choose with our mind or with our heart. Is it possible to choose with both or are they forever separated by the sword?

This card represents a choice to be made. More importantly, it represents different ways to make decisions. When this card comes up in a reading, you are being asked to consider carefully how you make the important decision before you. Do you follow your heart? Do you do what makes sense? This card suggests that there is a way to marry the head and heart so that wise, balanced decisions can be made.

If reversed, this card warns of making an unwise or unbalanced decision.

Use your intuition

The trees represent the signs of the zodiac and the Knowledge of Good and Evil. How do those ideas relate to the conscious and subconscious?

How did the sword come between the man and the woman?

In traditional tarot decks, a guardian angel presides over the man and the woman. Here, we've used the moon instead. How does that change the card's meaning?

A woman, holding aloft a glowing wand, rides through a dark, foggy landscape that may or may not be treacherously dangerous. Pulling her and her chariot are two strong horses, representing great energy and power that she must control. They don't appear to be well trained, as they are not looking straight ahead but in different directions, as if distracted by the ravens and shadowy shapes in the mist. The chariot driver is using all her focus and will to keep the chariot on track.

This card is about victory through mastery. In this situation, there are opposing and conflicting forces, perhaps very powerful ones, that must be made to work in harmony to achieve a common goal. These conflicting energies may be within yourself or external. Either way, it is up to you to harness that energy and guide it to success.

If reversed, this card warns you against two possible things. First, beware of letting others take control of you. Second, there is a danger of you running over everyone in your path in your haste to reach your goal. It might be wise to slow down and see what lies ahead before you go barreling down the road.

Use your intuition

Is the chariot driver using reins or just her mind to control the horses?

What do the ravens represent here?

Where is the chariot driver going on this dark, foggy night?

A woman sits fearlessly next to a roaring lion. Although the lion—who is very large and very powerful, with very large, sharp teeth—could destroy her instantly, she seems unconcerned. Behind them is a fiery landscape representing a situation requiring great courage. By wearing virtually no clothing, the woman indicates that she is very comfortable with herself. The lion is her own inner animal instincts and passions. She is not afraid of them nor does she seek to control them by physical dominance, but rather with a gentle understanding and acceptance. Instead, she sits confidently with them, recognizing them for what they are. She can use this inner passion as she wishes instead of being controlled by it or repressing it.

This card is about understanding your drives and passions. By understanding and accepting them, you can use them to achieve your goals. You can become so self-possessed that you move through your life with a quiet strength that doesn't need to exert itself needlessly, but is always ready when needed. This card suggests that now is a time to exert that quiet, yet undeniable, strength.

If reversed, this card warns of two things. Beware of letting your animal passions and instincts control you. Beware, as well, of repressing or denying them altogether. Either extreme will cause problems.

Use your intuition

Why is the lion roaring?

Is the woman looking at the lion or at something off to the side? What does she see?

This woman has tamed the lion so it doesn't attack her. Would it attack someone else?

An old man, a hermit, stands on a stone arch in the midst of a bleak landscape. He has removed himself from society to seek answers within himself. He uses a glowing wand as a staff and also clutches another staff topped with a snake's head. Nearby are books, representing the knowledge he has gathered through study. The atlas is a record of the many journeys he's taken and the experiences he's gained. The Tree of the Knowledge of Good and Evil in the background also speaks to his vast experience. He has, in his day, eaten quite a few metaphoric apples. The magnifying glass symbolizes closely examining all beliefs to see if they are good ones. The pencil and paper show his desire to keep a record of his findings, so that nothing is lost due to forgetfulness. Also, he values clear and concise thought and practices the motto, "Writing makes an exact man." The Hermit uses these few humble items to review and assess everything he's ever learned, thought, felt, and experienced, in order to understand his own beliefs and to seek truth.

This card is about seeking truth. Not the intuitive truth of the High Priestess and not the learned truth of The Hierophant. The truth you need is your own truth. You need to withdraw from the situation for a time. Use this time to review all your knowledge, understanding, and experience. When you figure out how it all works together, you will have the answer you need.

If reversed, this card warns of withdrawing too much, or for too long, or for the wrong reasons. Spending time alone in order to avoid people, put off making decisions, or procrastinating is not going to serve you well in this case.

Use your intuition

The Hermit clutches a tall staff with a snakehead on it. What does it symbolize?

The Hermit stands on an impossibly constructed stone arch. Why is it constructed like that? The arch so seems small—is it going over the ground, a stream, a deep crevice, or something else?

A cold-faced stone Sphinx stands guard over a wheel with mysterious symbols on it, including astrological glyphs indicating the role of the stars or fate in the affairs of humans. The bleak image is softened somewhat by the presence of three women. We would be mistaken, though, to seek comfort from them, for they are the three Fates, Clotho, Lacheis, and Atropos, who spin, measure, and snip the threads of our lives. In the center of the wheel is the sun and moon in all its phases, representing the cyclical nature of life and, indeed, of fate. What we have here is a sign of change beyond our control or even our ability to anticipate.

This card represents an unexpected change in your plans, a conflict of interest, or an idea ready to materialize. Whatever happens will be beyond your control. This card advises you to get ready for something new. Don't be rigid with your plans at this time, but prepare to go with the flow. It is likely that the temporary chaos will bring good fortune in the long run. Events will unfold in such a way that it will be impossible to miss the hand of fate in your affairs. Be ready to make the most of it.

If reversed, this card can suggest a temporary setback or even a complete reversal of fortunes in a direction that you didn't desire. It can also warn against the uselessness of flailing in the face of circumstances you cannot change.

Use your intuition

The sphinx stares directly ahead; is it looking at you or elsewhere? Why?

None of the Fates look at the reader. Why not?

The Fate in the red cloak, Atropos, the cutting of the threads, is facing directly away from the reader through a stone portal. What does that symbolize?

At the base of stone stairs, between two pillars, Justice stands, holding a gleaming sword, its point resting on the ground. In her other hand, she holds a set of scales before her. The sword with its point on the ground indicates that Justice grounds her decisions with proper discrimination and consciousness. The pillars represent the conscious and subconscious, meaning that our actions and our intentions are considered as Justice makes her decisions. The scales weigh our decisions and the outcome used to determine our future. This is the role of Justice, also known as

Karma, for she is universal justice. Her judgments and her application of justice maintain the fairness and justness of the universe. Our choices and our actions have consequences, and Justice determines exactly what those will be.

This card represents the importance of your choices. Whatever decision or decisions you make now will have significant consequences in your future, so choose carefully. Rely on logic and reason to make the decision, rather than emotion. If you are experiencing good fortune, this card can be letting you know that your past actions made the good fortune possible. It could represent a legal situation that will be resolved in your favor. This card is also a reminder to balance your physical concerns with spiritual growth.

If reversed, this card suggests that you are experiencing less than good fortune because of your decisions in the past or that you are in the process of making an unjust decision or one based on emotion rather than logic. It can also point to a legal situation not in your favor.

Use your intuition

What does the swirling pool of water at Justice's feet symbolize?

Where do the stairs behind her lead?

If our actions, decisions, and choices go in one side of the scale, what goes in the other?

Two ravens watch as a woman hangs upside down, suspended between two living trees. Turbulent waters rush below her, but she appears perfectly at ease, almost as if she were meditating and not suffering. This woman is hanging here voluntarily. It is easy to imagine that before assuming this position, she practiced fasting and other forms of physical denial in order to seek a spiritual experience. Her efforts are successful, as can be seen by the glowing radiance around her head. Hanging tranquilly between earth and sky, in a place between worlds, she is experiencing things that she'll never forget and that will change her life. In this state, her day-to-day hopes, desires, and goals no longer seem important; her only focus is on spiritual enlightenment.

This card can represent, very simply, sacrifice. You may be asked to give up something for the sake of someone or something else. This card can also indicate the need for a change in thinking or a new point of view. Or it can be a more spiritual activity, one where you give up something of yourself to gain spiritual wisdom. It can also mean, almost literally, a time of suspension, a time where you should do nothing at all.

If reversed, this card suggests that you are being asked to make a sacrifice that is too big and potentially harmful to you. It also implies feeling confused—as though your world has been turned upside down—thereby making you immobile, unable to take any action.

Use your intuition

Why is the woman dressed as she is? What do the black gloves imply?

What exactly are those ravens doing there?

There are grapes growing on the left tree. What does that symbolize?

A figure cloaked in black, holding a scythe, whom we can only assume is Death, sits on a pile of skulls. A white rose, symbolizing new life, grows from the base of the skull pile. A young girl sits nearby, next to a tree stump, mourning her loss. Death and the girl are together on a small island, indicating that the great loss of death can make one feel alone. However, while the island is surrounded by water, there is other land within view, reminding us that the sorrow of death does end and we will return to our everyday lives again. Although not as bright as usual, the sun is rising in the distance, barely shining through the clouds. Above the island, a ghost of a woman floats upward. Her arms are outstretched and her head thrown back as if in relief and joy, as if she were released, at last, from something painful.

This card can, but rarely does, refer to physical death, which is some comfort. Death, though, whether physical or metaphorical, is not an easy experience. This card implies the end of something, perhaps a job, a relationship, a situation, an organization. The actual ending will likely be hard, but once it's over the cycle continues and something new will come. On the other hand, it may be a welcome closure, such as ending a bad relationship, quitting an unhappy job, or selling a house to get a new one. On a spiritual level, this can mean a symbolic death where you eliminate old beliefs that no longer work for you and perhaps were holding you back. Death is usually hard, but it must happen before transformation or resurrection occurs.

If reversed, this card can imply resisting death and perhaps even stalling it. Letting something drag on beyond its natural life span leads to stagnation.

Use your intuition

What is the story of the woman and the little girl? Are they mother and daughter, the same person, or is there some other relationship?

Is Death hanging around the girl, or has the girl sought out Death?

The moon shines down on a serene scene as a woman sits peacefully in the midst of some rapids. Although the water rushes around and under her, she is unaffected by it. She holds two chalices, pouring water from one to the other. Despite the churning chaos around her, she pours perfectly calmly, nothing disturbing her. This is the simple and elegant message of Temperance: to remain perfectly balanced and centered, no matter what the circumstances. This card is about balance, but not necessarily the way we think of balance. It does not mean equal amounts of everything all the time. It means remaining perfectly balanced, no matter what else is going on, which means Temperance is always in motion to adjust to changing environments and situations. Sometimes she needs to pour a little more out of one chalice, sometimes the other—it all depends on what is going on around her.

This card suggests that you watch your balance. Take the time to make sure your reactions, decisions, and words are appropriate for the situation at hand. You are advised to practice moderation and patience. This is no time for extreme behavior or melodramatic gestures.

If reversed, this card implies someone whose behavior is out of control and very clearly immoderate. It can, although rarely, suggest that an extreme stance is called for.

Use your intuition

What is the white flower to the left and what does it signify?

What happens when one of the cups is emptied of all the liquid?

This scene is set at night. How would the card's meaning change if it were daytime?

A pale woman is chained, hands and feet together, and left on top of a huge horned skull. The horns are a sign of masculine virility, yet they adorn a dead skull. She, too, is crowned with horns as well as jewels. Both she and the skull are surrounded by flames, representing passion. She is, it appears, enslaved by her passions. She doesn't act afraid or even interested in getting away. Her expression looks almost amused. It is easy to assume that she is here of her own free will. However, as time passes and the flames grow and perhaps other uncomfortable situations develop, she may find she no longer has a choice, that she cannot get out of the situation without help. A pentagram represents the four elements under the dominion of the spirit. However, the pentagram on the skull is inverted, signifying the dominance of the physical world over the spiritual one.

The Devil card is rarely a pleasant one. It suggests bondage or addiction to a dangerous practice, substance, situation, or person. Less extreme and less dangerous, it can represent overindulgences of any sort—eating, drinking, sexual activity, staying up late, etc. These may be unhealthy and the appearance of this card in a reading may remind you to adopt more moderate practices. Being held captive by your passions might feel like fun for a short time, but such imbalance is never a good long-term plan.

If reversed, this card can indicate a close call with resisting temptation or eliminating certain pleasures from your life for fear of becoming addicted. Also, this can represent a recent release from a dangerous or destructive situation.

Use your intuition

What is the raven doing there?

Could she, or would she, ask the raven to bring help?

What is the significance of the moon in this image?

On top of a stony hill stands a delicate, glass-domed tower. Two sides are supported by sculptures of human figures. The moon is perfectly positioned to shine through the sides of the tower. This lovely structure is hit by lightning and destroyed. The tower represents material ambition, ego-driven thinking—or a faulty belief system, relationship, or way of life. The lightning is an event that causes spiritual insight, which leads to the destruction of false thoughts, beliefs, and practices.

This card's simple image indicates a major change in your life or belief system. Be prepared for emotional upheaval and distressing events. This bolt from the blue, this event will create a spiritual epiphany that will allow you to eliminate all that is no longer useful or good for you. Lies and half-truths will be revealed. It is a sort of purification. Whatever is solid and good will remain. You will have a foundation that has survived trial by fire and you can rebuild with confidence, once the dust has settled.

If reversed, this card implies that the shakeup caused by the Tower is not external but rather internal and less obvious. Instead of a storm, something happens inside you that creates the epiphany.

Use your intuition

What do the figures on the sides represent?

This tower has a glass dome. Is that significant?

What willl remain of this Tower?

Moonlight dapples a tree and reveals an ibis, representing pure, focused thoughts, a quiet presence overlooking the scene unfolding on the riverbank below. A woman emerges from the river, reaching toward a butterfly—a symbol of transformation—that is just out of reach. On a jutting bit of rock, another bird observes. Overhead an eight-pointed star that represents the creative and regenerative energy of the universe shines predominantly in the sky. In the background, barely visible, is a constellation of a pentacle. Here, the pentacle represents the five senses. Because the pentacle is dim, it indicates that reliance on the senses should be less at this time and, instead, focus on the regenerative energy of the universe should be highlighted.

In the face of troubling events, the Star offers hope and guidance. As you emerge from troubled waters, you will find clear signs directing your path. Now is the time to stop focusing on what has happened in the past and look instead to the future. The universe is offering refreshment; a transformation is at hand. You just need to reach out and take it. Even if the evidence of your senses indicates otherwise, focus only on the hope that is provided. Steer your actions by the light of the shining star and you will soon be on solid ground.

If reversed, this card suggests that signs from the universe are being overlooked. Everyday events are distracting you from your true path.

Use your intuition

There is an urn on the riverbank. Has the butterfly just emerged from it? If so, what are the implications?

A second bird sits nearby. What does it indicate?

A full moon looms over a raging body of water, a shadowy presence illuminating challenging times or perhaps a troubled soul. Two identical towers representing good and evil frame the scene. A wolf and a lobster guard a stairway, the only visible means of crossing the turbulent waters. The lobster, a creature from the murky depths of the ocean, indicates deep fears. The wolf, untamed and wild, represents the spirit, unbroken and strong. The stairway is close to the water's surface, barely providing safe passage. The journey may be dangerous and frightening, but it must be made. Only by facing fears can progress be made.

The Moon is at once dreadful and beautiful. It represents dreams, instinct, intuition, and fears. Its gentle light provides both illumination and shadows. This light can cause things to seem either safer or more dangerous than they actually are. Be prepared to be both frightened and inspired. Carefully separate your intuition from your fears and follow your intuition. Pay careful attention to your dreams at this time. Great inspiration is at hand, but it won't be an easy journey.

If reversed, this card warns of deceptions, dangerous emotional swings, and giving in to fears. Tread carefully.

Use your intuition

Is the wolf there to guard the path or to guide you across it?

Why does the path pass through the middle of towers representing good and evil?

The face in the moon is gazing to the left. How is that significant?

A pale woman stands as if amazed by her surroundings. She wears heavy clothes and furs as if she was just transported from a bleak, frigid landscape into this bright, temperate new place. A warm sun shines softly over the meadow where sunflowers, daisies, and wildflowers flourish. A stone arch leads away from the meadow toward a tree.

The Sun brings a simple message of joy. After traveling through the long, dark night of soul searching, you emerge into the light. All your journeys, all your spiritual seeking, all your sincere efforts now pay off. You are able to see where you were and where you now stand. Your mind is clear and sharp. Energy fills you and you are ready to let the light of the sun warm you. This card brings great joy, clear truth, and well-deserved success. It also indicates music or science or anything requiring sound reasoning and logic.

If reversed, this card suggests too much of a good thing. Too many projects and too much energy can lead to burn out. Over-thinking or analyzing is a danger. It can also indicate that something is blocking the usual happiness and success that the Sun brings.

Use your intuition

The woman in the card is gesturing toward something we cannot see. What do you think it is?

The face in the sun is looking toward the right. Compare it to the face in the moon. How do the different directions affect the cards' meanings?

What happens next in this image? Does the woman go through the stone arch toward the tree or toward whatever she sees to the left? Why? What does she find there?

A star shines, sprinkling its rays softly over an angel sounding a trumpet. The angel floats over churning water. Shapes and figures seem to emerge from those waters. The music from the trumpet calls up troubling and disturbing possibilities, and yet the overall feeling of the scene is peaceful and safe. The angel appears approachable and soft, but she exudes a quiet power and strength. Her wings are large and promise the ability to float above the troubled waters.

Judgement provides a call. You are being called to face your past before moving on. It is time to acknowledge whatever has happened, accept it, and let it go. You have learned so much and been through so much, you now have the wisdom and strength to free yourself from the past. A time for change is at hand—perhaps a new job, a new relationship, or a new way of life. However, unlike other cards indicating change, in this case you are more in control. You've decided to heed the call. You have the experience and the knowledge to move forward. You just have to make your final farewells.

If reversed, this card warns of hanging on to the past and using it as an excuse to not move forward. Similarly, it can mean moving forward, but dragging the past with you.

Use your intuition

Is the angel in any danger from the images emerging from the water?

What would happen if the emerging images touch the angel? Would they be transformed? If so, how?

A woman holds a veil that seems to capture and disperse starlight as she moves it about. She dances at the top of the world in celebration, for she has conquered all that she set out to do. She is surrounded by creatures of air, land, and sea, representing all that she has achieved. The sea creatures symbolize her emotions, dreams, and fears; the flying creatures, her mind and thoughts; the land animals, her ability to move comfortably and confidently through life. The light within her veil shows that she can access and use the energy of the universe.

This card, the last Major Arcana, is about big achievements. The World promises the wonderful conclusion of long-term projects and the realization of goals. Success, completeness, satisfaction, and fulfillment are woven into your life. This card can also indicate major trips and extensive travel.

When reversed, this card indicates the delay of achievement. Success is still possible, but something is in the way. This could be as simple as refusing to accept success. Similarly, it can suggest that travel plans may be postponed.

Use your intuition

There are different creatures on this card: a tiger, a lion, a stag, an eagle, a dolphin, a fish, and a butterfly. What could each of them symbolize?

Do you see any other creatures not mentioned above?

Notes

_____
_____
_____
_____
_____
_____
_____
_____
_____
_____
_____
_____
_____
_____
_____
_____
_____
_____

The Minor Arcana

These cards remind us of the humble deck of playing cards. They are familiar and comfortable. In their images, we recognize the events of everyday life, from having a busy day at work (Three of Pentacles) to getting that promotion (Six of Wands) to being worried about that fight we had with our best friend (Nine of Swords). Within these cards you will find the patterns of your life.

Notes

_____

_____

_____

_____

_____

_____

_____

_____

_____

_____

_____

_____

_____

_____

_____

_____

Wands

Your passion, your drives, your ambitions—these are what you will find in the fiery wands. Images of new jobs, angry fights, parties, and victories flow through these cards. When they appear in your readings, expect lots of energy.

ACE OF WANDS

A glowing wand, alive with growing vines and leaves, has split a rock, indicating that a new path is open. The castle in the background promises great things to come.

This card indicates a creative opportunity. This is an excellent time to harness the energy and passion that this opportunity brings and use it to take the first steps toward your castle—whatever form that castle takes. You recognize this opportunity and can feel the excitement within. Take it and run. It's a magical moment and won't last long.

If reversed, this card suggests an opportunity missed or one that should probably be passed on at this time.

Use your intuition

What is the woman doing in this card?

What does the split boulder represent?

What is the raven's role in this image?

A magician holds a wand while trying to summon the other wand to him. The two wands and the twin arches represent two possible projects or directions. The water and the moon in the right archway promise that by trusting your instincts, a wise choice can be made.

The Two of Wands suggests the need to choose between two ventures. In this case, either option requires your full passion and attention. This is not the time to split your focus and your energy. Although both choices are appealing, go with your instincts and you will make the right choice.

If reversed, this card can indicate that you are unable or unwilling to make a choice. It can also represent being faced with two unappealing choices and feeling forced to pick the lesser of two evils.

Use your intuition

An open box is at the magician's feet. What's in this box?

A raven perches in the left arch. What does it suggest?

3 OF WANDS

A woman stands on the shore of an ocean, waiting for something. She has set up her wands along the shore, indicating that she has initiated a project. Now she waits for initial feedback or reaction to her new venture. A crescent moon hangs low in the sky. The moon, mostly hidden, suggests that much is still unknown. The woman does not know if her efforts will pay off, yet it is easy to imagine that she is visualizing her ships coming in.

This card indicates great vision and foresight. You have taken an idea and started implementing it. You have laid the groundwork for a new business, enterprise, career, or project. You can clearly see your goal. Take a step back and watch for initial responses. Because you've done your work well, you can expect to see signs of success.

If reversed, be prepared for a delay in the expected returns or perhaps responses that are not quite what you've hoped for.

Use your intuition

There is a tree on a cliff to the right of the woman. What does it signify?

Two of the wands are topped with silver symbols, but the third one is not. Why is that?

A happy couple celebrates under a structure made of four wands and beautiful green boughs—their efforts have been crowned with success. Sheaves of wheat are at the base of the wands, indicating abundance. A raven perches above them with a bit of clover in his beak.

This happy card represents a moment of celebration. Whatever you've been working on is showing good signs of success, so take a moment to revel in it. In fact, things are looking so well, you can use some of your gains to lay a foundation for the future, whether it's building a house, expanding your business, investing, or even getting married.

If reversed, this card warns you not to celebrate too soon. Things appear very fine but you need to wait a bit to make sure. It can also suggest that you rethink your plans for the future.

Use your intuition

There is a castle in the background. What is its significance?

The raven holds a three-leaf clover. Four-leaf clovers are good luck, so what is the message of the three-leaf clover?

In a clearing in the woods, on a cloudy moonlit night, five women wield wands. Their wands represent their energy, their passion, and their interests. They are in a competition of some sort, but not a battle to the death. Whoever can use her wand most effectively will prevail.

The Five of Wands is a card of combat, competition, and strife, so be prepared. In this situation, different people bring their different agendas and desires. Not all can be accommodated, so they have to fight it out to see what will be kept and what will be eliminated. You need to understand and respect your competition, to be confident in what you are fighting for, and to conduct yourself with skill.

If reversed, this card suggests that this is a fight that you shouldn't get involved in. Assess your motives and the competition before rushing in. It can also indicate a competition that is less than honorable or one that turns ugly.

Use your intuition

Why have these women decided to conduct their competition at night?

Do the different manners of holding the wands and the different stances suggest ways of approaching a competition or fight?

Are there any rules to the women's competition?

A knight rides his armor-clad horse through a meadow carpeted with wildflowers and wands alive with new growth. His helmet feather is a bit bedraggled, indicating a hard-fought battle. His wand is topped with a wreath of victory. He has, indeed, faced a tough fight, but he has come through victorious and is humbly receiving recognition for his achievement.

This is a card of victory. Whatever you have set your hand to will prosper and you will be happy with your success. It will be personally satisfying but it will also be crowned with public recognition in some form. The acknowledgment will make this moment even sweeter.

If reversed, this card can indicate not receiving the accolades you expected and think you deserve. It can also mean the victory achieved did not bring the satisfaction you thought it would.

Use your intuition

The knight and his horse are clad in black. We usually think of heroes dressed in white. Does the black affect your response, or interpretation of this card?

The raven on the back of the horse has a tired, crestfallen air about him. What role does that have in a card of victory?

A determined warrior stands on a hill. She is clearly ready to defend herself and her turf. Beyond her is a vast expanse of land and water, a very lovely landscape. This indicates that she has a lot worth defending.

With this card, someone or something has put a block in your path. Before you can move forward and continue on your journey, you have to face a challenge. You need to be brave, strong, and confident. This is not a fight to ignore; there is too much at stake. You cannot afford to give up. You must defend yourself.

If reversed, this card asks you to consider what exactly it is that you are defending. There is the possibility that you are wrong and should lower your defenses.

Use your intuition

Compare this card to the Five of Wands. How are they similar and how are they different?

There are six other wands in this image. Are they all hers? If not, are they those of people she's defeated or of her comrades who have abandoned her?

A woman sits, ready to jump up and be off at a moment's notice. She watches to the right while eight wands fly from the left toward whatever she is watching. In the distance is a ship.

This card is full of fast-moving potential. Like the woman in the card, you need to be ready to spring into action. Whether you've set up things ready for action, or you've been watching for your opportunity, the moment has come. Things may seem chaotic, but just jump in, maintain your focus, trust your instincts, and you should do well. This card can sometimes indicate getting news or information you've been waiting for or quick, unexpected trips.

If reversed, this card suggests that you are being hasty. You are moving too fast and are not in tune with the energy surrounding the situation.

Use your intuition

What does the woman see?

Is the ship in the harbor coming or going? How does that direction, one way or the other, play into the meaning of the card?

The raven sits on the top wand with a rather jaunty air. What does he symbolize here?

Awoman stands under an arch examining a wand. The wand and the others in the background are starting to blossom but the woman looks dissatisfied. She seems to be wondering how much longer she'll have to wait before they bear fruit.

This card implies that you are tired; no, you are exhausted. You can't imagine going on one more step. But the Nine of Wands encourages you to do so. Not only are you almost there, but you do indeed have the strength to get there. Tap into that core of determination you have and make that final push. All that you've set out to achieve is just within your grasp.

If reversed, this card suggests that you've invested a lot in something that turned out not to be worth it after all. It can also indicate that there is nothing you should be doing, just step back and let time do the rest. In this exhausted state you are likely to make a mistake.

Use your intuition

What could this woman be doing to help the wands grow?

Why has she pulled one from the garden and moved it closer to the structure?

A man struggles across a field as he carries a large bundle of wands alive with new growth. The turret of a castle can be seen far off on the horizon. Wildflowers and butterflies adorn the field, although the man is likely unaware of this beauty.

This card is, in a way, a victory. It signifies that you've achieved your goals. However, it also indicates an ending. This phase of the project is over. You cannot continue on in this manner; it is just too much work. Now is the time to scale back on your workload. Downsize the project. Delegate tasks. Hire more staff. Ask for help. Do what is necessary to lighten your workload.

If reversed, this indicates not that you've taken on too much, but have shirked your responsibilities. If you don't pick up your fair share, someone else is going to have to.

Use your intuition

What do the wildflowers and butterfly represent?

What is the significance of the new growth on the wands?

What is the man's relationship to the castle on the horizon?

Notes

_____

_____

_____

_____

_____

_____

_____

_____

_____

_____

_____

_____

_____

_____

_____

_____

Cups

Your emotions, your creativity, your dearest relation-ships—these are what you will find in the watery cups. Images of new loves, celebrations, dreams come true, loss, and happily-ever-after flow through these cards. When they appear in your readings, expect to feel the emotional highs and lows of life.

A woman embraces a large stone crowned with a beautiful chalice overflowing with water. The five streams of
water represent the outpouring of spirit over the material
world. A dove, symbolizing the descent of spirit, drops a
wafer into the chalice, a gift of pure love.

This card presents the gift of love. This can take the form
of a new romantic interest, a creative desire, or a spiritual
awakening. At this time, your life is filled with possibilities
and abundant, joyful emotions. All you need to do is embrace

the moment and use that energy for the start of something wonderful.

If reversed, this card suggests feeling depleted, empty, and very much in need of spiritual or emotional refreshment. It can also represent the opposite: feeling overwhelmed and drowning in emotions.

Use your intuition

This card is very dark on one side and very bright on the other. What is the implication?

What does the moon symbolize in this card?

Standing in a lush, vibrant landscape, a couple gaze into one another's eyes as they toast each other and their relationship. This is a happy picture of a loving relationship. Above them floats a caduceus, indicating that together they form something that is stronger than the sum of their individual selves.

This card promises a strong and passionate relationship. Such a relationship brings beauty and power to life. While this can be a romantic relationship, it can also mean any such union of people, groups, ideas, or talent. The key here is the coming together of two things that creates a third thing that is, in and of itself, powerful, beautiful, and passionate.

If reversed, this card can indicate a union or partnership that in theory or on paper should be amazing, but the reality is that there is just no emotional connection.

Use your intuition

He is toasting with his left hand; she, her right. Does this have any significance?

Likewise, he is nearly naked while she is clothed and even wears a scarf. What are the implications?

A full moon shines through a rainbow-hued sky upon a field of wildflowers creating a scene of magical vibrancy. Amongst the flowers, three women dance with their cups held high, their contents spilling over them, symbolizing their outpouring of emotions, friendship, and affection.

This joyful card represents a time of celebration and mutual support. It is the grateful recognition of family, friends, and community and all that they add to our lives, often in the form of holidays, birthdays, anniversaries, or other celebrations. The Three of Cups can suggest the ending of disagreements by way of a happy compromise. It is an all around good omen in financial, relationship, work, or spiritual concerns.

If reversed, this card can indicate that support systems, friends, or family have let you down or that a party or celebration will not go on as planned.

Use your intuition

On the left, a raven sits on a pumpkin. What does this symbolize?

The three women are all different ages. Does this affect the meaning of the card?

A pale woman sits under a tree, knees drawn up, and arms clasped around them. She has cut herself off and has turned completely inward. Nearby sit three cups that she seems to want no part of. In the distance is a cup on a stone, overflowing with water—something worth having, if she'd only look. Farther back are a stag and a castle. Just above her head in a notch in the tree perches a small owl, the promise that wisdom is available.

This card represents self-absorption, apathy, and boredom. You have been disappointed by somebody or something and now you are emotionally stuck. You don't like what's in front of you and you can't be bothered to look further than your own brooding mind. It is a shame because, if you listen to the voice of wisdom, you will look up and see that what you need is not far away.

If reversed, this card can mean a deeper depression or engaging in unhealthy activities to relieve boredom.

Use your intuition

Around the base of the tree, mushrooms are growing. Do they add anything to the meaning of this card?

A stag and a castle are visible in the distance. What do they symbolize?

In this image, what do you think happens next?

A woman wrapped in a beautiful cloak stands facing us. Her expression is one of pain, but with a touch of strength and bravery. Three spilled cups lie near her, while two full cups are behind her. She has suffered a loss and feels great pain. But she is not destitute by any means. In the distance are a castle and a harbor with a ship in it. Two bridges promise to make the journey to the castle shorter and a little easier.

This card shows a time of difficulty and loss. More specifically, it is about how you deal with that loss. Every loss initiates change and is an opportunity for growth. Loss hurts because of our emotional resistance to change. This card represents that moment. But it carries a word of advice: look at the wonderful opportunity around you and move forward.

If reversed, this card can indicate an out-of-proportion reaction to loss, real or imaginary, for the sake of melodrama or attention.

Use your intuition

Does this woman live in the castle or is she just making her way there?

What does the swan in the middle of the lake symbolize?

A mother and a child, representing an innocent, loving relationship, stand together amongst cups filled with beautiful, colorful flowers. Behind them is an interesting round structure. Against the murky sky and landscape, the woman, child, and flowers provide a welcome splash of color.

This is a card of sweetness, kindness, and innocence. The Six of Cups brings with it memories of happy times in the past. It can represent a time of sweet, simple joys or it can be something larger. Perhaps a passionate pursuit or beloved creative endeavor that you let go of will return to your life. It could be a harbinger of someone from your past whom you would welcome back into your life.

If reversed, this card can be taken two ways. Perhaps you are wrapped up in nostalgia and cannot move ahead or feel satisfied because nothing will ever be as good as what you remember. Contrarily, it can indicate that you do not remember your past fondly and that you don't want anything from your past to visit your present life.

Use your intuition

The mother is showing the girl a vase of flowers, yet the girl seems only interested in the flower she is holding. How do you fit that into the meaning of this card?

Do the different flowers or colors of the flowers have any symbolic meaning?

At the edge of a rocky shoreline, a woman sits, staring up at seven magnificent cups, all filled with different beguiling treasures. She is emotionally drawn to each one and cannot make up her mind which to take. The water and the moon in the background both accentuate the emotional pull that these dreams have over her.

This card represents having too many choices, all of which seem very appealing to you. You are spending time dreaming about them, imagining what each would be like. Still, you cannot pick one. This card includes a hint that might help. You are drawn to these choices emotionally. Set aside those emotions for a moment and invite a little reason into the picture. While emotionally appealing, some of the choices may not be good for you. Choose wisely.

If reversed, this card indicates someone who is living in a dream world without any real choices, just fantasies and hopes.

Use your intuition

What does each treasure in each cup represent?

Which tarot card would correspond to each treasure?

A woman carrying a violin and a lantern turns her back on eight cups. Either the moon or the lighthouse is beckoning her, compelling her to leave her past behind and strike out on a new journey. The image has a feeling of melancholy; there is sadness that she is leaving, but it seems like it is inevitable.

This card represents a very small but powerful moment in time. You've decided you need to leave something comfortable behind and you have come to terms with that. You've decided what dream you're moving toward. This moment, the one where you finally turn your back forever and before you take the first step, is the Eight of Cups. It can be such a conflicted moment, filled with sadness over leaving, yet knowing you are doing the right thing.

If reversed, this card suggests that you've given up the dream and decided to stay put, whether you are fulfilled and satisfied or not.

Use your intuition

Do you think the moon is leading her or the lighthouse? Why?

She is carrying a violin and a lantern. What do they symbolize?

What does the daffodil near the cups signify?

A dreamy woman sits on a stone throne. A unique round window is framed by nine gold chalices. A bouquet of yellow flowers brightens up the room.

This card is one of happy contentment. Things are good and you like them that way: friends, family, feasting, fun, creative fulfillment, and satisfying work. Your life is full and you are enjoying every aspect of it. This card is often called the "wish card." It's true; you feel like you have all that you could wish for.

If reversed, this card indicates that your fondest wishes and desires are not coming true. It could indicate the unraveling of a happy life or a major aspect of it.

Use your intuition

The woman is sitting on a stone chair. Why?

What do the yellow flowers represent?

A husband and wife embrace under a rainbow. Their child is nearby and in the background is their castle, shining bright and beautiful.

This card hardly needs any explanation. It is nothing more and nothing less than an ideal family life. For you this can mean just that. Or it can represent the components of such a life: a safe, comfortable place to live and people, either friends or family, to share your life. It's about having people to share your joys and support you through your sorrows.

If reversed, this card warns that all is not well. Someone or something is disrupting the happy home. Or an important component to your family life is missing.

Use your intuition

Has this couple been together for a long time? How can you tell?

Have they faced troubles together or are those yet to come?

Notes

Swords

Your intellect, your thoughts, your fears—these are what you will find in the airy swords suit. Images of problems solved, heartache, battles, and escape flow through these cards. When they appear in your readings, expect to be challenged.

A sword embedded in a stone glows in a dark landscape. A crown rests on the top of the hilt, representing the supremacy of clear thinking and rationality, the crowning glory of the gift of swords. A woman lightly touches the sword and experiences a powerful spark of illumination.

The Ace of Swords is the gift of knowledge and understanding. You can expect a flash of insight or an idea that will help solve a particularly sticky problem or experience a moment of truth. If you want to communicate something with clarity and just the right words, the energy to accomplish that is present at this time. It can also represent a new point of view, discovery, or intellectual achievement.

If reversed, beware of the double-edged nature of the sword. This card can indicate a painful truth or sharp, cutting words. It can also suggest that you should let go of an idea.

Use your intuition

What do the red roses climbing the sword symbolize?

What is the significance of the cross at the top of the crown?

A blindfolded woman wearing vibrant red sits on a bench with two perfectly balanced swords symbolizing a difficult decision or conflict. The moon hangs in the sky, illuminated by a curious beam of light. Behind her, a turbulent ocean churns and rages, a sign of her emotions. Two ravens sit quietly, watching to see her next move.

This card represents a difficult situation. You are dealing with two conflicting ideas or a challenging decision, but you are not willing to face the situation. You've closed your eyes to it. Rather than view it rationally, your emotions are distracting you. The Two of Swords suggests that this situation would benefit more from a rational decision than from an emotional one. It can also represent a truce or stalemate.

If reversed, this card indicates a broken truce or an imbalance in the situation. It can also mean that a choice is made *for* you rather than *by* you.

Use your intuition

What is the significance of the beam of light and the moon?

What is the role of the ravens in this image?

A woman lies, worn out with pain, beneath a huge heart stabbed by three powerful swords. The points of entrance are a brighter red, signifying the newness and rawness of this wound.

The Three of Swords is one of the dreaded cards in a tarot deck. Life does sometimes bring us these moments and this card signifies that. It represents a new, raw pain. It can be a major situation, such as finding your lover unfaithful; or a smaller one, such as cutting and hurtful words from a trusted friend. Swords represent truth and this is a case of the truth hurting very much indeed.

If reversed, this card can represent pain based on a misunderstanding or malicious gossip. It warns you to make sure you know the full truth of a matter, as the matter may not be what it seems and someone may be trying to hurt you cruelly and needlessly.

Use your intuition

The woman lies on a blue blanket. How does this affect the meaning of the card?

Although the heart is pierced, no blood drips from it. Why not?

Beneath a lavish stained glass window, a woman rests with her arms crossed over her chest. Four swords hang on the walls around her, representing the problem or problems that surround her. The situation still exists but she has, for the moment, removed herself to a quiet, peaceful state of being.

This card suggests that you have situations, troubles, or problems that need resolution. However, this is not the time to deal with them head on. Rather, it is a time to take yourself away, calm down, and heal a bit, so that you can approach your issues refreshed. Quiet, peaceful reflection and meditation will bring clear insight so that you can handle the situation to your benefit.

If reversed, this card indicates a willful and unproductive ignoring of a situation. There is no refreshment, no insight. Instead there is either denial or useless obsessing.

Use your intuition

The window above the woman depicts the story of the shepherd finding a lost lamb. How does this play into the meaning of the card?

One sword is hanging upside down. What does this signify?

On the banks of an ocean, a defiant-looking woman stands, surrounded by swords. Two other women run away from her and seem to be following a raven toward a ship off in the distance.

This card represents the end of an argument or clash of some sort. The winner is ambitious and may have won by aggressive or less than honorable methods. It indicates a situation where someone has put her needs above the needs of others and is concerned only for her own interests. You will know if you are the winner, or the one running away.

If reversed, this card suggests an empty victory that was not worth the energy and consequences.

Use your intuition

The women appear to be running toward the ship in the distance. Is it in a bay? How will they get to it?

A bit of light is peeking out from behind the moon. What does it represent?

A woman sits in a boat while another woman deter-minedly guides the boat through the water. Six swords are in the front of the boat and the passenger hunches up as if having a hard time looking at them. In the distance, a castle sits at the top of a hill.

This card represents moving from rough waters to smooth. You are leaving a bad situation and heading toward resolution. Although you are headed in the right direction, the Six of Swords reminds you to remember the troubles you've gone through and to learn from them. They are all opportunities for gaining wisdom. This card can also suggest a trip or change of scenery.

If reversed, this card can indicate letting someone else make your decisions or tell you what to do. It can also mean that you are moving in the wrong direction.

Use your intuition

What is the relationship between the two women?

A raven sits on the hilt of one of the swords. What is his role in this image?

A woman wearing a jeweled headpiece sneaks around outside an encampment, gathering swords. She looks up, as if caught by surprise, doing something she shouldn't be doing. She has left two swords upright in the ground, indicating that she is picking and choosing the ones she wants.

The Seven of Swords indicates the potential for thievery, sneaking about, and trickery. Someone involved in the situation has decided to use subterfuge to achieve his or her goals, which may or may not be honorable. A strategic plan has been devised and enacted and will likely be successful, at least as a means to an end.

If reversed, this card warns that such a tricky plan will not work out and whoever attempts it will be exposed.

Use your intuition

Who lives in the tents and what is this woman's relationship to them?

She leaves two swords behind. What do they symbolize?

A woman is loosely bound and surrounded by swords, symbolizing being trapped and immobilized by a situation. She seems to sway and moan, bewailing her situation without making any real progress. In front of her, there is an opening in the circle of swords, representing a means of escape. Far above her, on a hill, a castle is silhouetted by the moon.

This card represents a situation in which you feel helpless. Problems surround you. You feel trapped and that no matter where you look, danger, obstacles, and problems confront you. The card also suggests that while the situation probably is as bad as you think, escape is possible.

If reversed, this card suggests that the feeling of entrapment is in your mind. You thought about things in such a way that they've become traps and dangers, but they either aren't real or aren't what you've made them out to be.

Use your intuition

Is the castle a place of safety or something else she needs to escape?

The swords are embellished with gold leaves. What do they symbolize?

A woman sits up in bed, hugging her knees and burying her head against them, clearly tormented by her thoughts, represented by the swords floating above her head. She is not covered, showing how vulnerable she is at this time. A white teddy bear and a box are hidden under the bed.

This card is about those worries that keep you up all night or wake you suddenly in the early morning hours. Thoughts, worries, guilt, anguish, or concerns fill your mind and create havoc. You seem unable to settle your mind. The lack of sleep adds to the situation, making you feel even more vulnerable.

If reversed, this card suggests the possibility of full-blown insomnia or the use, and perhaps abuse, of sleep-inducing drugs.

Use your intuition

There is a white teddy bear under the bed. What does it symbolize?

A box is hidden under the bed. What is in it?

A woman crouches on a stony beach, ten swords stabbed into her back all along her spine. She looks like she is trying to get up or just unwilling to fall all the way to the ground. Sunlight shines through the clouds over a still and peaceful ocean, symbolizing a calmness of emotions that seems at odds with the destruction on the beach.

This card says in no uncertain terms that, finally, it's over. You have fought and worked at it, but you cannot change the situation; there is no fixing it. You may want to try one last time, but you will have to accept that this time you are beaten. It's a strange moment because you thought you'd feel a lot of more pain and distress, but actually you feel calm and peaceful. Deep down, you are relieved that you don't have to fight it anymore.

If reversed, this card indicates that although the situation is over, you refuse to accept that fact and are continuing to fight and cause yourself more pain than necessary.

Use your intuition

Although the woman is stabbed with swords, there is no blood. What does this suggest about the nature of the situation?

The image is bleak, but there are a tree and a castle in the background. How do they play into the card's meaning?

Notes

Pentacles

Your money, your resources, your health—these are what you will find in the earthy pentacles. Images of skills acquired, money gained and loss, gifts received, and sensual pleasures flow through these cards. When they appear in your readings expect cash to flow, one way or the other.

An ornate pentacle rests in a flowerpot upon a stack of stones. Flowers spring from the pot, indicating abundance and beauty. On the stones, berries represent fruitfulness and a butterfly shows transformation. A vine circles the pentacle, further symbolizing growth. A woman at the gate turns, as if just in time, to notice this gift that she may have overlooked.

This pentacle brings with it the gift of luck, an opportunity for material gain, or improved health. It is solid and grounded and represents something practical and dependable. This is the seed of good things to come. Use the energy of this moment to start a new project, make a small investment, or start a fitness program. You have the opportunity to grow something wonderful. This card can also represent the arrival of some unexpected money or material item.

If reversed, a moment of bad luck may be at hand. Something you were waiting for did not come or something you planned did not take root and grow as planned. It can also indicate that you are overlooking something that could be useful to you.

Use your intuition

Unlike in the other aces, the woman here is far away from the pentacle. Why?

A fence surrounds this symbol. What is the implication?

A woman stands on a shore juggling two pentacles, symbolizing multiple tasks that require attention. Two ships are tossed on stormy seas, showing that things are rough, but if handled skillfully, everything will turn out fine—after the bad weather passes. The blue sky on the horizon indicates that the storm will end.

This card promises busy times ahead. You will have a lot going on and multiple things, such as projects, financial concerns, or health issues, to juggle. It suggests that being flexible and going with the flow will help you keep all the balls in the air. It may be dangerous or challenging, but this is a temporary situation. Maintain your focus and it'll be over soon enough.

If reversed, this card suggests that too much is going on for you to handle it all well. You may drop a ball or something might fall through the cracks.

Use your intuition

If water suggests emotions or intuition, what is the role of the turbulent ocean here?

A shadowy image of a serpent entwines itself between the two pentacles. What does it symbolize?

Awoman works on a painting under an ornate arch topped by three pentacles. Two women stand nearby watching and admiring her work.

This card is a sign that all is going well. If you have started a new business, embarked on a new project, or begun a health or fitness routine, you are seeing the signs of progress and even of prosperity. You've paid attention and done the best that you can. You are getting attention and probably reimbursement for your work. Not only is the external recognition satisfying, but you are also finding much personal fulfillment in your endeavors.

If reversed, this card suggests that things are not going according to plan. Maybe you've taken on too much and cannot handle everything very well. Or it could mean you haven't applied yourself as well as you could have.

Use your intuition

One of the women watching holds a parchment. What is written or drawn on it and what is its significance here?

There are three pentacles, two candles, and one ladder. Do these add meaning to the image?

A woman sits on the ground in front of a bench, clutching a pentacle tightly to her chest, indicating that this is something she holds very dear. A pentacle is behind her adorning the bench while two statues stand on either side. She has a bench but refuses to sit on it, suggesting that she won't use what she has. Two warped pentacles lay before her, symbolizing her twisted attitude toward them.

This card represents a miser. You may have plenty, but you are afraid to use it, share it, or enjoy it. Something is threatening you, whether your own fears or someone trying to take what is yours. You are so afraid of losing what you have that you hold it too close. Your attitude toward your gifts, whether it is your money, your belongings, your time, or your health, has become twisted, controlling, and unhealthy.

If reversed, this card suggests the opposite. You are giving away too freely, spending too much, or overindulging in other ways. It could also mean you are trying to take something that isn't yours, causing someone else to hold tightly to it.

Use your intuition

What do the statues on the bench signify?

A calm river can be seen in the background. Is this woman on a bridge? If so, what does that imply?

Two people, poor and destitute, linger outside a church door. One, who is perhaps lame, sits on the ground with her hand outstretched, seeking donations. The other turns away, throwing a proud and stubborn look at passersby. Although in front of a richly decorated door, neither consider knocking.

This card indicates going through rough times, either physically or financially. That is hard enough, but this card carries a more distressing message. You are letting these hard times erode your spirit, your faith, and your desire. You don't have the energy to get through this time. You have no faith that things will turn around. You don't even desire to seek the help that may be available.

If reversed, this card indicates that you no longer linger outside but rather that you do seek help and take advantage of opportunities to turn this situation around.

Use your intuition

The standing woman wears a black cloak lined with red. What does that red lining symbolize?

If the women knocked on the door, what would happen next?

In the middle of a courtyard, a woman stands, holding a scale. Before her are two beggars. She gives money to one. It seems the other is to be denied any charity.

This card deals with giving and receiving. Depending on your situation, this card can have different meanings. If you have a need, that need will be met by gift, donation, or through some unexpected source. If you are seeking aid, such as a scholarship or loan, this card is a favorable omen. If someone approaches you for help, you will find yourself in the position to provide it.

If reversed, this card suggests that your need will not be met, the loan or scholarship denied. If you are approached for help, you will be unable to do so. It can also indicate that you will be offered help but will refuse it.

Use your intuition

One woman is dressed in white, the other in red. What does this signify?

The woman receiving the money is wearing a large gold pendant. Why is she asking for money?

A woman stands before a bush heavy with pentacles. She holds a hoe and stands as if waiting; it is nearly time for her harvest. She uses this moment to reflect on her efforts, assessing whether the energy she put in is worth the results she'll get.

This card tells you to take a break. You've done all you can do for now. Just like this farmer who has planted, weeded, and watered, you must wait for time to do the rest. Neither you nor the farmer can force that. This card indicates that your careful efforts, planning, resourcefulness, and research will pay off. When the harvest comes, it will be a good one.

If reversed, this card indicates that you've moved too soon and hence the harvest will not be all it could have been. It can also mean that, despite all your best efforts and timing, the harvest will not be successful.

Use your intuition

A raven perches on the top of the bush. What's his message to the farmer?

How does the full moon in the background add to the meaning of this card?

A woman works in a studio with a breathtaking view, symbolizing that her work has given her a new outlook on life. She hangs pentacles on the wall, checking for errors and painting them over and over again if necessary to make sure that she learns how to do it just right. She works long into the night, representing her commitment to her new art.

The Eight of Pentacles is known as the "apprentice card." It means you've taken up a new job, craft, art, or activity. It's not an easy road, for being a beginner brings a hard learning curve and tedious repetition until you get it perfect. Because you have a goal and the passion that comes with a new endeavor, it's likely the bumpy, beginning part of the journey will not discourage you.

If reversed, this card can suggest that you being a nitpicker, too much of a perfectionist, or perhaps a workaholic. It can also mean someone who is finding his or her job boring and tedious.

Use your intuition

What does the red trim on her dress indicate?

What is the significance of the four candles—why not three or five?

A bird perches on the hand of a woman standing in the midst of her garden. Bright sunflowers bloom all around her. Grape vines are heavy with fruit. In the distance is a large, elegant house. The bird represents spirit, which the woman values most of all, in spite of her great material gain. She has accomplished much because she has listened to her spirit and followed her heart.

This card represents the achievement of good things. Not only have you prospered, but you've done so in a way that you feel good about. You appreciate and cultivate the best of everything life has to offer, physically, intellectually, emotionally, and spiritually. This card can also indicate the enjoyment of simple but decadent physical pleasures and treats.

If reversed, this card still indicates achievement, but it may not be as fulfilling. Either the means to the end was not satisfying, or you find yourself alone and lonely, with no one to share your material gains.

Use your intuition

Why are grapes and sunflowers used to represent her achievements?

The woman's hair is extraordinarily long. What does this symbolize?

Aman and woman dance together, their faces filled with joy, as pentacles sprinkle down around them. They have a good, strong home already and in the distance another ship is coming in, promising even more wealth. They not only have enough, they have more than enough.

This card represents a strong, secure foundation, usually based on family ties, whether a home or business. It also deals with legacies, received and given. You may either receive a legacy or small winnings to invest for the future. Or you may acquire a home or business of your own, creating security for you and your loved ones. Another possibility is investing in the community in some way, through a scholarship fund or civic improvement. This card could play out several ways, but however it does, it'll be good, prosperous, and beneficial to you and your loved ones.

If reversed, this card forewarns of a legacy, investment, or financial security that is lost, possibly through the market, legal fees, or taxes. It can also mean an expected inheritance did not turn out as you'd hoped.

Use your intuition

There are two dogs near the couple, but no children. Why?

Who is that woman in white holding the blue-tipped staff?

Notes

The Court Cards

These cards resemble the royalty cards in a deck of playing cards, but represent so much more. We see people that we know, like our mom (Queen of Cups), our boyfriend (Knight of Wands), and our sister (Page of Swords). Within these cards you will find the people who influence and affect your life…or perhaps even aspects of yourself or different roles that you play.

We'll start with the pages, followed by the knights, then the queens and finally the kings.

A woman stands, holding a wand. She is gazing downward, focusing, as if trying very hard to keep still.

This page indicates a creative restlessness, pent-up energy, and perhaps some frustration. She has passion and desire, but she just isn't quite sure how to put it to good use. This is someone on the verge of a discovery or new phase of life. The sooner she is able to start that new phase, the happier she will be. Pages also represent messages. In this case, possibly a message about a new job or career, travel, or something of a spiritual nature.

If reversed, this page represents someone who is expressing her pent-up and frustrated energy in inappropriate and possibly destructive ways.

Use your intuition

What do the purple flowers in her hair symbolize?

What is the significance of the bleak landscape?

PAGE OF CUPS

This woman dances on a shore beneath a rainbow. She holds aloft a simple chalice containing a fanciful blue fish. To us, it is a cup and a fish; yet she sees worlds of wonder in the smallest things.

This page is sweet, sensitive, and creative. She is a dreamer, the type of girl that enchanted fish tell stories to. Her life is filled with rainbows and magic. She is intuitive and emotional. She loves openly and deeply. Perhaps she gives a bit too much of herself and risks getting hurt. She is constantly being inspired and is always on the verge of some new project or creation. That story the fish told her? She'll write it, illustrate, hand-bind the book, and give it to that nice woman she just met the other day. Pages also represent messages. In this case, possibly a message about a loved one or a creative project or possibly a love note.

If reversed, this card represents someone who is overly sensitive, whose feelings get hurt at a drop of a hat, or a very moody person who has no appropriate outlet for those strong feelings.

Use your intuition

What does the rainbow symbolize?

The woman is on a rocky shoreline. Is she in any danger?

This woman holds a sword close, as if embracing a problem or challenge. She looks at some exotic red flowers,
undoubtedly finding the inspiration she needs to solve her
dilemma.

This page is insatiably curious. She wants to know everything. She can be infuriating and annoying, but she can also
help open up your thinking. With all her questions, she is
perfect for problem-solving and out-of-the-box thinking.
She can be an over-achiever or a slacker, if not properly challenged. Her mind is brilliant and sharp, but she does lack in-

tellectual discipline. Pages can also represent messages; in this case, a message about a problem, a solution, or gossip.

If reversed, this page still wants to know it all, but is more interested in knowing things she shouldn't or that others would rather she not know. She is not likely to keep any secrets, no matter how much she promises to.

Use your intuition

Birds are flying in a "V" formation in the sky. What does that signify?

There are some white flowers behind the page. Do they represent something that she might be overlooking?

PAGE OF PENTACLES

This woman holds a pentacle that she has just ornately embellished. She admires both the final product and remembers with pride her industrious efforts in creating it.

This page is industrious, crafty, good with her hands, and very earnest about saving her money. She likes to learn new things and particularly enjoys structured learning, classes, workshops, and programs. She is clever and creative in finding little ways to earn money or supplement her income. Always seeming to have a little something extra, she is generous and often gives unexpected gifts. Pages can also represent messages; in this case, a message about money, resources, a material matter, or a health issue.

If reversed, this page can be someone in a position of servitude or under someone's control. She can also be someone who is stingy and a penny-pincher, or who never wants to give or do more than she has to.

Use your intuition

She is wearing a red gown and a fur-trimmed green cloak; is there any symbolic significance?

Do you think she has just made the pentacle or is she analyzing it to determine how it was made? How would that answer affect this card in your reading?

KNIGHT OF WANDS

A man kneels while gazing up at the ornate and living top of his wand. Even though he is kneeling, his energy and desire to get moving is almost palpable.

This knight is impetuous, impatient, generous, and ambitious. He is willing to go anywhere and do anything and is happiest when he has a clear goal. He is probably very popular and the type of person people like to be around. He is given to grand gestures that spring from the best intentions; for example, he'd give the coat off his back, even if it leaves him without a coat. But he can be undependable. Because he is impatient and impetuous, he can lose interest in the task at hand and run after the next shiny new challenge.

If reversed, this represents someone prone to making foolish choices, who thinks only of himself, or always has to be the center of attention.

Use your intuition

The wand is alive and growing. What does that symbolize?

There is a castle in the distance. Has he come from there or is he going there?

This knight moves gently and quietly through a twilight landscape. He is in no hurry, for he is probably lost in his own world of dreams. There is nowhere he would go that is as satisfying as the romantic realms of his fantasies.

This knight is the quintessential romantic knight in shining armor. He is chivalrous and romantic and fiercely loyal. He's dreamy, appealing, sensitive, and emotional. He loves art and has a deep appreciation for all beautiful things. He's always a bit of a distracted day-dreamer. He may not take action because he is too busy dreaming. He may be too shy to ask you out, but once he takes you out, he'll make you feel like a princess. Common sense is probably not one of his virtues.

If reversed, this card can indicate someone who is prone to depression or moodiness. He may sink into gloomy pessimism and brood.

Use your intuition

His horse is draped (the other knights' horses are not). Is there any significance in that?

Why do you think he carries the chalice in his hand instead of packing it safely in a bag?

This energetic young man is riding furiously toward an unseen foe. As he brandishes his sword, the tip catches the moonlight. He moves with the self-assurance of one who knows exactly what he is doing.

This knight is single-minded and intensely focused. He knows what he wants and is certain he knows how to achieve it. His intellect is stunning, and his mastery of language is a thing of beauty. He is very confident in his opinions and beliefs and loves to express them in friendly but no-holds-barred debates or arguments. If you need someone to advise you about a logical problem or plan, you can count on him. Do not, however, go to him with problems of the heart; he is generally impatient in the face of emotions.

If reversed, this knight can be a braggart or even a liar. He will tell stories to bolster his own self-esteem and to gain the respect of others. He lacks compassion and takes pleasure in verbally embarrassing people.

Use your intuition

The tip of his sword catches the starlight. What does that suggest?

There is a sign to the right. What does it say?

This knight enjoys the finer things in life, as seen by his elegant plume and velvet cloak. He has a clear goal, the delivery of the pentacle. He will not cut corners or look for shortcuts, but travels slowly and carefully until he reaches his destination.

This knight is the most dependable of the knights. You can count on him to do what he says and to do it well. Whatever the task at hand, he'll work until it's finished. He's the handyman who can do anything. He's the kid who works his way through school and manages to save for his house at the same time. He's good about saving and investing carefully, but he's not about making a quick buck or taking big risks. He is extremely organized, maybe annoyingly so. He can be a loner, preferring staying home to nightclubs or large parties. He is sometimes a little too cautious in his choices and a little too tight with his money. He can be dull and stubborn.

If reversed, this knight is downright cheap and boring. He might be slightly obsessive-compulsive or antisocial. He certainly won't do anything for free, so don't ask for any favors.

Use your intuition

Where is he taking the pentacle?

He doesn't appear to have any weapons. Is he in danger of being robbed?

QUEEN OF WANDS

This woman holds a living wand, showing her dynamic energy. A sunflower nearby indicates her optimism. She wears a yellow gown, the color of fire and energy.

This queen is energetic, creative, dramatic, faithful, and warm. She lives a busy life and seems to accomplish everything with style. She is outgoing and has a natural interest in people. New activities and challenges delight her. She's not afraid to try anything. Her wonderful characteristics benefit those around her and she can be a transformative force in the lives of others. She is a natural leader and loves to plan and organize events.

If reversed, this can represent someone given to melodrama, or someone who can be very bossy or controlling.

Use your intuition

What is the role of the cat in this image?

Her throne has a sphinx on either side. What do they represent?

QUEEN OF CUPS

This woman sits in a beautiful seaside garden. Lovely colors and elegant forms delight her beyond all else. She gazes dreamily at an ornate chalice, lost in her appreciation and seeing things others probably miss.

This queen likes to make a pleasant place for people to gather and wants everyone to be comfortable and happy. She is very sensitive to others' feelings and often knows when something is wrong before they do. She usually knows just what can help the problem, too. She can be quiet and shy, but once engaged in a conversation she is a good and caring listener. She is kind, gentle, and nurturing. As a lover of the arts, although perhaps not an artist herself, she encourages the skills and talents of others. Her psychic abilities can be very strong. She can be moody, depressed, or overly introverted.

If reversed, this card represents someone who can be controlled by her emotions, and become obsessive or manipulative. She may play the victim a little too readily.

Use your intuition

A *boat glides through the water behind her.* What does it symbolize?

What does she see as she gazes at the chalice?

This woman sits on her throne, waiting for the next great conversation or problem that needs solving. Her sword is ready and sharp, and she is most comfortable when she can use it.

This queen knows a lot, from personal experience, from extensive reading, as well as from observing life around her. She can, if she wishes, chat with anyone about almost anything. She can fit comfortably in almost any situation. She can see the big picture surrounding a problem and can tactfully but forthrightly give a solution. She loves to help and share what she knows. She enjoys intellectually stimulating pursuits and makes a good, loyal, and interesting friend. However, she can appear to lack affection or emotional warmth; some find her intimidating and unapproachable.

If reversed, this queen is cold, judgmental, and harsh. While extremely smart, her gifts are tarnished by pain and bitterness; she tends to use her knowledge and her tongue to cause unnecessary pain.

Use your intuition

She dresses in black, but sits among colorful flowers. Why?

What do the mountains behind her represent?

This woman drapes herself prettily over her throne, wearing a gown probably of her own creation. She gazes downward, either assessing the design of her skirt or mentally rearranging the basket of fruit into a more pleasing composition. While she does enjoy the beautiful things around, she loves to find ways to improve them.

This queen is very down-to-earth. Something bothering you? She'll offer fresh-baked cookies or a pot of soup. She loves to garden, cook, bake, sew, do-it-yourself projects, or anything that can make her environment more beautiful, comfortable, and efficient. And she is very good at every-thing she does. She loves to make plans and lists, and loves even more to cross things off those lists. She is practical and efficient. She can run the perfect household or a successful business with equal grace. While she enjoys external recog-nition, she gets even more satisfaction through accomplish-ing her projects. She can become too focused on the material world. For example, in trying to create the perfect birthday party, she may neglect the little birthday girl who wants to help.

If reversed, this is a queen who may sacrifice her own joy and other people's feelings in favor of practicality. She may try to meet emotional needs with material items. Her dedica-tion to her lists and timeline make her rigid and unable to respond with flexibility to the needs of others, or perhaps even to her own needs.

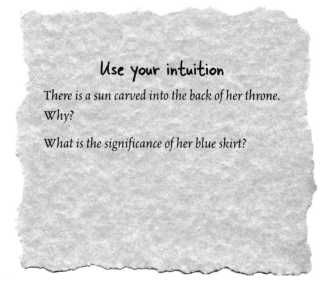

Use your intuition

There is a sun carved into the back of her throne. Why?

What is the significance of her blue skirt?

This man has charmed a lion and lioness, who are content just to be in his presence. A light burns at the top of his throne, for he is always filled with ideas and energy. Although he is sitting now, he is only waiting for the next opportunity for action.

This king is passionate and he leads with confidence and energy. His natural charisma and sense of fun motivate all who follow him. He somehow convinces his followers that they can accomplish anything and they love him for giving them that feeling. He is not one to go with the flow. Instead he sets his own goals and makes his own way toward them. He can charm almost anyone into doing almost anything.

If reversed, this card can represent a demanding and impatient tyrant. He can be someone who pouts and becomes jealous when he is not the focus of attention. He can also have anger issues.

Use your intuition

What do the lion and the lioness symbolize?

The wand he holds is alive with red berries growing on it. What is their significance?

KING OF CUPS

This man relaxes on his throne on a platform near the edge of the sea. No matter what turbulence goes on around him, he is relaxed and able to enjoy what life has to offer.

This king is peaceful, sensitive, affectionate, and calm. He loves his home and values family and a relaxed home life. He prefers to lead by teaching through gentle guidance. He may enjoy expressing himself creatively, but is even more supportive of others' creativity, sometimes at the expense of his own. He is generally friendly and caring, a very nice man to have around. He can be overly sentimental and may seem "soft" to those who don't know him well.

If reversed, this king can mistreat his family members in the name of love or deny problems or issues rather than address them. He may be prone to over-indulging his habits, good or bad.

Use your intuition

What is the role of the ship and the eagle in the background?

What do the shells at the king's feet symbolize?

This king sits with his preferred tools (or weapons, depending on your point of view), an incredibly bright sword and a magnificent hawk. These indicate his sharp intellect that always goes directly to the heart of any matter.

This king leads by intellectual ideals. He does not seek to inspire passion or have his people love him. He uses intelligence, objectivity, and analysis to decide what is right, fair, and just. These are the ideals he upholds for himself and for those around him. He leads by example. His standards are very high; he expects a lot of those around him. He has no patience for anyone who doesn't do their best or who doesn't share the same ideals. He can lack compassion for what he may perceive as weakness and is intolerant of uncontrolled emotional outbursts.

If reversed, this king may use his impressive abilities to further his own agenda with no respect for ethics, standards, or ideals. He can be ridiculously judgmental and hold people in contempt if they don't behave or think as he deems appropriate or right.

Use your intuition

This king is very much about intellect. What, then, does the moon in the background suggest?

There are three trees in the background: one blooming with flowers as if it were spring, one red as if it were fall, and one green as if it were the height of summer. Why?

KING OF PENTACLES

This king sits amidst all his abundance. He has created a strong, beautiful home and is proud and protective of it. He will play the host gracefully as long as he is sure his stability and security are not threatened.

This king is practical, hard working, and steady. He is ruled by common sense and practicality. He loves the simple comforts of home and family. He can be a very social and welcoming host, inviting anyone who enters his home to share a meal. Although he enjoys the company of others, he is very self-contained and likes to rely on no one but himself.

He is generous with his money and resources, but never stupidly so. He is reliable and will always keep his word. He can seem to lack affection and is not one to share his feelings, even to those closest to him.

If reversed, this king can be stingy to the point of cheating someone. He can be erratic, demanding, and callous. He may resist change and make it difficult for those around him to try new things.

Use your intuition

Three candles burn at his feet. What do they symbolize?

This king has woven vines into his crown and hair. What is the significance?

Notes

Notes

_____

_____

_____

_____

_____

_____

_____

_____

_____

_____

_____

_____

_____

_____

_____

_____

About the Author

Tarot, oracles, and magic have all influenced Barbara's life for more than a decade. She has studied under some of the most influential tarot experts in the world and continues to teach and work with some of the brightest stars in the field.

Barbara enjoys the challenge of giving a voice to tarot cards and oracle decks. She has had the good fortune to write books for several decks, including A Guide to Mystic Faerie Tarot (Mystic Faerie Tarot), The Gilded Tarot Companion (the Gilded Tarot), The Witchy Tarot (The Hip Witch Tarot), and Destiny's Portal (The Enchanted Oracle).

Free Catalog

Get the latest information on our body, mind, and spirit products! To receive a **free** copy of Llewellyn's consumer catalog, *New Worlds of Mind & Spirit,* simply call 1-877-NEW-WRLD or visit our website at www.llewellyn.com and click on *New Worlds.*

LLEWELLYN ORDERING INFORMATION

Order Online:
Visit our website at www.llewellyn.com, select your books, and order them on our secure server.

Order by Phone:
- Call toll-free within the U.S. at 1-877-NEW-WRLD (1-877-639-9753). Call toll-free within Canada at 1-866-NEW-WRLD (1-866-639-9753)
- We accept VISA, MasterCard, and American Express

Order by Mail:
Send the full price of your order (MN residents add 6.5% sales tax) in U.S. funds, plus postage & handling to:

Llewellyn Worldwide
2143 Wooddale Drive, Dept. 978-0-7387-1436-3
Woodbury, MN 55125-2989

Postage & Handling:

Standard (U.S., Mexico, & Canada). If your order is:
$24.99 and under, add $3.00
$25.00 and over, FREE STANDARD SHIPPING

AK, HI, PR: $15.00 for one book plus $1.00 for each additional book.

International Orders (airmail only):
$16.00 for one book plus $3.00 for each additional book

Orders are processed within 2 business days.
Please allow for normal shipping time. Postage and handling rates subject to change.

Mystic Faerie Tarot
Artwork by Linda Ravenscroft

BOOK BY BARBARA MOORE

Step inside the enchanting world of the fey. Rich watercolor images by renowned artist Linda Ravenscroft capture the vibrancy and grace of faeries, sprites, elves, and nymphs in their lush gardens.

Each suit tells a "faerie tale" as the nature spirits embark on magical adventures. A water nymph and wood elf learn that love is a gift not to be taken lightly, while a foolish faerie queen and her kingdom are nearly overtaken by a magical blue rose. These stories offer lessons and fresh insights in all matters of life, while remaining true to tarot archetypes.

The *Mystic Faerie Tarot* kit includes a 288-page book that introduces tarot and describes the major and minor arcana in detail. You'll also find faerie-themed spreads to use, along with sample readings and a quick reference guide to the cards. Perfect for beginners.

ISBN: 978-0-7387-0921-5 $24.95
Boxed kit (5½ x 8½) includes an 78-card deck, 288-page book, and an organdy bag with a satin cord.